From Chrysalis to Butterfly

by

Anna Delves

A personal journey revealing how knowledge of our past lives can heal us today and divulging some of the hidden depths that lie between us all.

authorHOUSE®

AuthorHouse™ UK Ltd.
500 Avebury Boulevard
Central Milton Keynes, MK9 2BE
www.authorhouse.co.uk
Phone: 08001974150

First published by AuthorHouse 7/9/2008

ISBN: 978-1-4343-9100-1 (sc)

Printed in the United States of America
Bloomington, Indiana

This book is printed on acid-free paper.

Foreword

I HAD NO IDEA THAT I was about to write a book. The universe certainly sprang the idea onto me as I lay dying in hospital in September 2007. I found that words and sentences were pouring into my head to such an extent and in such a professional style that they had to be coming from someone other than me.

As soon as I left hospital I could hardly wait to get a piece of paper out and start writing. I was physically weak, totally unable to look after myself in any way, but yet after two days I could balance a lap top on my knee and type for an hour or so at a time. I never spent time thinking about what I would write each day, I didn't have to. As soon as I opened the computer the words just flowed out.

In four weeks, the essence of the story was on computer. I felt so relieved. The effort had been enormous and I felt as if I had been living on a different planet for a whole month. After this, the insistence to write every day was lifted from me and I was able to rewrite what had been channelled through me in a more leisurely way, making it more understandable and correcting my mistakes. I was never allowed to alter the content, even though I tried several times to add other events in. The initial channelled writing was the story that had to be told and nothing else would do.

Contents

Introduction

THIS NARRATIVE WAS PLANNED BEFORE I was born and it feels as if I, and my family and friends, have been acting out a play that was always going to happen. As with Jesus, who's story was written many centuries before it took place, I, as an old soul, had agreed to live this 'play' a long time ago, and there has never been a moment when I was going to stop it happening, however painful. Its purpose is not to recount a harrowing tale for you to 'ooh' and 'aah' over, but to bring understanding to those who are ready to hear, of how our past lives are intrinsically linked to our present lives. It is part of the universal plan that we awaken to a greater depth of knowledge at this time, and to start taking greater responsibility for who we really are.

Everything that I have recounted is as close to the truth as I can get it from my point of view. Out of respect for my family and friends, I have given everyone false names. There are many events over the years that I have not included, but I have been guided so precisely in writing this, I am sure that all that the universe means to be included, is included! This story of how two life times interrelate has taken just under twenty years to unfold. Several other life times have also been revealed to help in the untangling of the same web. If there is anything more to unfold, which there may well be, it is obviously not ready to be related at this time.

There are in fact three stories unfolding throughout the book. One reveals the untangling of a particular past life with this life and all the healing that understanding it has brought. Another is the telling of how an ordinary family home was destined to become a spiritual retreat/sanctuary. The third is the unfolding of my own life and how it has always been designed to bringing about the first two stories.

It is important to appreciate the fact that my husband was the physical aspect of putting me to death in a past life and that he was instrumental in saving my life in this one. I feel quite awed by the fact that something happened deeply within him as he put me to death and he recognised that I was, after all, a good woman. It has never been revealed to me just exactly how he knew this, but I do know that he spent the rest of that life investigating who I was and what I stood for. I feel even more awed that, around three hundred and fifty earth years later, he reincarnated with me again, married me, and worked unbelievably hard in the years that we were married to improve himself. It has become increasingly obvious to me that he elected to do this and it is very humbling to know that he so willingly saved my life in my darkest hour when I was very close to death, despite the fact that we were no longer together as a couple. I hope you will perceive the beauty of this as you read the book.

The story I have related to you is probably the base story of us all, if we did but know it. However we each dress our own stories in our own choice of clothing. When I disowned Jesus at his crucifixion, through intense fear of being put to death, some two thousand earth years ago, I allowed the serpent to embed itself deeply in the core of my being. I then righted the wrong that I had done to Jesus when I was put to death as a witch, because I died upholding my love of God and did not shrink from losing my life for him. I did not however, get rid of the fear that had taken a hold of me at the crucifixion and that was making me, from the moment I was born in this life, believe that I was such a 'bad person'. This fear has dogged me throughout this life and probably many others in between, stopping me from holding my head up high and being the real me. I have allowed people to walk all over me and I have cowered under attack! But, during a recent illness, I was shown how to overcome the serpent by loving it and my fear no longer had a foothold. I am learning not to cower any more, and I am intent on restoring myself to full spiritual health.

It is wonderful to have such 'in depth' knowledge of how karma works. Most of us are working out just such karma in our everyday lives and we do not recognise it. Hopefully, after reading this book, you will start to recognise your own patterns and look at your own family, friends - and even those who you do not care to call your friends - in a new light. Certainly most of them will have gathered round you for a very good reason and your so called 'enemies' may often be such because they hold some of the most 'painful' clues to your growth.

If I have one big frustration about earthly life, it is the continual feeling of being inhibited by my body.

This is unfortunately a necessity of humanness but I am forever trying to push its boundaries as I walk my path. I would love to be a part of bringing some of the boundless freedom and knowledge that death brings us all, down to the earthly realm.

Enjoy my narrative. Ask to learn what YOU need to learn as you read it, for my story (clothing) is not yours; but it may trigger something that will help you to understand your own life. Remember that I am only a human being and as such have picked up the threads of the past lives as truthfully as I can. As you read on, however, you will see much evidence of the past lives borne out and from this I take great encouragement. My only worry in putting my story into book form is that the human language can be so inadequate. But I have done my best!

The most humbling thing of all is knowing that this book is only a tiny stepping stone towards human awakening and that in the next couple of generations its content will be 'old hat'. Our children and our children's children understand so much more than we did at an early age, as the wheel of evolution spins ever faster.................

1

The Early Years

I WAS BORN IN 1956, into an affluent and well to do family. My father was a naval officer and my mother was a very dutiful officer's wife. Shortly after I was born we were posted from Worthing, Sussex to Amersham in Bucks where I spent my first five years very happily. I was always very independent; my mother frequently told the tale of the day she lost me, before I could even walk. I was found crawling down the avenue in my nappy and very little else, as fast as I could!

My earliest years were spent in the company of my two sisters, one who was three years older and one who was three years younger and as far as I can recall we were extremely happy. I have only two memories that blighted those days. The first was of little bouts of completely overwhelming misery that suddenly came upon me for no apparent reason. I can remember going up to my bedroom and howling my head off, and when my mother came in to ask what was wrong I used to say to her,

"I am such a bad person, I am so, so bad!"

And I remember vividly how black everything felt around me. My mother would hold me and talk to me until I calmed down and recovered.

The second was my intense fear of water. I remember screaming whenever I was taken to the seaside and was forced to approach the enormous, splashing waves.

In 1961 my father left the Navy and took a job in Edinburgh. We bought a house about eight miles south of Edinburgh and spent the next three years of our lives amongst the Scots, acquiring broad Scottish accents and enjoying the hard frozen winters, learning to ice skate on the rivers. I have few significant memories of those days but one that still sticks out in my mind is that of my elder sister and I being bullied mercilessly by local village children, both on our way back from school on the bus and as we walked up the lane to our home. I had no idea at the time why it was happening, but looking back at it now, I think it must have been because we were dressed in school uniform and therefore were not, 'one of them'. This was the first time that I became aware that not everyone in the world was friendly.

We had a young Dutch au pair in those days who was very fond of us and took us everywhere, but I recall that she wasn't especially honest. Somehow she allowed my sister and me the freedom to steal some goods from the local shop. I remember my sister took some items of food and I somehow obtained a packet of plasters, but my memory is very vague as to exactly how it all happened. Anyway, in my complete innocence, I put a lovely round plaster on my leg and felt very grand! Later that evening when my mother was bathing me, she saw the plaster and asked where it had come from. I don't remember what I said to her but I do remember feeling very hot and uncomfortable. And so the story came out and the next thing I can recall is my father giving my sister 'the hair brush'. Whether I was deemed to be too young to be blamed I do not know, but I cannot remember being punished. My mother duly marched my sister down to the local shop the next day to give the goods back and to make her apologise to the shop keeper. I know, from subsequent conversations with my mother, that the aftermath of talk in the village cost our family reputation very dear. But my mother had done the right thing! This was how she brought us up – total honesty, at the cost of all else, was paramount.

When I was eight, the firm that my father worked for in Edinburgh went bust and my father was made redundant. My parents decided they would like to try and buy a farm and spent long hours away from home, looking at various possible properties in and around Wales and Gloucestershire. After one particular trip, they came back quite excited about a farm in the heart of the Cotswolds. My father travelled south again, intending to have another look at it. If he still liked it, the plan was that he should attend the auction that was to be held that same day. However, he was so delayed on the journey south that he had no time to revisit the farm before the auction, so he decided that he would go straight to the sale. He ended up buying the farm for twenty one thousand pounds, quite a sum in those days, and afterwards he set off for the property, to remind himself what he had bought! Apparently, when he got there he was horrified. The farm was much more run down than he remembered and needed a new roof to be even remotely habitable. He realised the enormity of the project that he had taken on and I was told by my mother that he really regretted buying it. But there was nothing he could do about it!

My mother however, on arriving at the farm, was absolutely delighted. She didn't care about the hardships we were to endure over the next few years; she had fallen in love with the place and it was a love that was to last for the rest of her life!

So my sisters and I found ourselves planted in rural Gloucestershire, never having had anything to do with the countryside before. We were placed in a local junior school and during the holidays were more or less left to fend for ourselves, whilst our mother and father attempted the mammoth task of trying to pull the old house and farm back into some sort of shape.

But life was good! It was full of new adventures and my elder sister and I romped over the local countryside, revelling in the new found freedom that we had and thoroughly enjoying all that nature was providing us with. A new phase had begun and it was to influence us for the rest of our lives.

At eleven years old I was packed off to weekly boarding school. I absolutely hated it for it meant leaving my pony and my beloved countryside and trying to fit in with the conventional patterns of most other children's lives. And I wasn't conventional!! All the girls at school loved putting on 'pretty' clothes, making themselves up, talking about boys, pop music, shopping etc. I was like a fish out of water. All I wanted was my home, my pony and my freedom. I started to get ill on Monday mornings and my mother had to get the doctor out frequently, to what I now realise were self induced panic attacks….manifesting at that stage as tummy upsets. My life became dogged with these troubles and I was taken to specialists all over the country to see if they could get to the bottom of the problem. None of them had any solutions that worked because in those days very little was known about 'emotional' upsets.

One amusing memory I have of my boarding school days was that of my 'magic pills'. My mother had given me some soda mints to take when I suffered from night time pains and she had put them in an old sweet tin with a very tight lid. They were harmless enough and simply served to shift any air that got stuck in my stomach. My friends used to watch me go to my drawer during the night to get a pill, and because I was a little embarrassed about it, I used to refer to them as my 'magic' pills. Somehow it came about that friends, who were struggling with an ailment of some sort, would ask if they could have a magic pill. I always gave them one and they tended to get better! I never told anyone what the pills really were and was secretly highly amused that they worked! It was my first introduction to 'mind over matter' and I was only twelve years old!

I finally left school at seventeen, throwing off the confines in which formal education had held me, with glee. The previous summer I had visited a family who lived in Annecy, France, whilst on a school French speaking trip, and we had got on extremely well. They had invited me to go and stay whenever I wanted to so, once I was free of schooling and I had managed to earn enough money for my air fare, I took off, much to my parents' concern. I left behind me all that was secure and loving and plunged into the unknown.

There then followed a six month period of total confusion. I became infatuated with the 'man' of the household in which I was staying and I succumbed to his needs as the innocent teenager that I was ......wooed by his French words and his promises. He swore me to secrecy over everything that was happening and I never even thought beyond the blissful moment of having a man 'wanting' me in this way. I allowed him all that he asked for and I expected no more from the world! During the day time I worked in various mundane jobs, trying to earn a bit of money to pay for my keep.

Then one night..... a night of horrors, I was woken up abruptly! My host and his wife were calling me from their bedroom and asking me to join them! I quietly got out of bed and stood shivering in their doorway, and was totally struck dumb, as they tried to persuade me to get into their bed with them. As they spoke my mind was racing, trying to comprehend that this man whom I adored, was actually asking me to share him with his wife in this way. I also gleaned that he would be making love to her while SHE would be making love to me! The shock to my innocent self was truly unimaginable and I broke down completely. I went into the bathroom and I sobbed my heart out. But thankfully, during that night, I started to see this man for whom he really was. Looking back, I feel proud that I didn't tell his wife about his real relationship with me because at that moment I felt he had utterly betrayed me and totally insulted my character.

After that night the relationship between us all

became pretty distant. I didn't leave the household as I had nowhere else to go and I was still a bit dazed from having my 'dream' life shattered. However, I started to find better jobs and a social life away from theirs. I gradually began to socialise with different people and to explore another world.

Unfortunately, exploring led me into all sorts of peculiar men's company and though I was wined and dined right royally, I did not realise the dangers of my association with such men and allowed them too much freedom of my body. Before too long though, I had had enough, so I decided to return home for a while to regroup with my family and friends. Therefore in July of 1974 I flew back to England, a very different girl from the one who had left six months earlier.

I can't remember being reproached for any of my actions when I arrived back home. Basically my parents were just relieved that I had returned safely and the talk was more about what I would do with myself in the future. The next incident I recall was sitting at the foot of my mother's chair one evening and casually stating that I might be pregnant. I don't think I really meant it at the time, but my mother got a terrible shock and started to ask me if it was possible. I didn't really think it was, but I remember being whipped off to the doctor (a family friend) the next morning and being forced to go into his surgery by myself, to tell him that I might be pregnant. My mother refused come in with me, she was too ashamed.

In the whirr of medical activity that followed, we discovered that I was indeed pregnant and I found myself being sworn to secrecy by my parents, being told not to tell anyone I was having a baby and to behave as normally as possible. Not long afterwards I was taken into a hospital to have an abortion. There were no ifs and buts about it. I had disgraced the family name, and taken us down to the level of the 'riff raff' down the road, of whom this sort of thing was expected. I was virtually MUCK! I don't remember much about the operation itself but I do remember waking up in the hospital after the abortion and screaming,

"Is it dead?"

And the nurses quietening me down and telling me it was all over. But it was in the moment of my scream that I truly became aware I had really had a life inside me and that it had been removed. Reality started to kick in for the very first time.

The days that followed were dark and I could liken them to living a terrible nightmare. I was taken back home to recover and I remember hiding from anyone who came to the door, not knowing whether to speak to them or whether I was even worthy of speaking to them. I had this overwhelming feeling of the disgrace I had caused and felt I was a totally dreadful person. I didn't feel I deserved to be a family member and thought everyone was looking at me in horror. It was as if fingers were pointing at me accusingly from every direction. I literally felt I was the worst person in the whole world.

A couple of months later my mother persuaded me to take a job in a hotel that was doing annual management courses. I think she saw it as a kind of halfway house…a place that was reasonably protected from the world, yet it had a management qualification at the end of it and gave me a small wage. I didn't much care what happened to me at that moment, so I agreed to go. The most important feature of that year, whilst I was trying to pick up the pieces of my life, was the fact that I met a fellow trainee student at the hotel who was later to become the best friend I could ever have. When I first saw her I admired her enormously and I was sure she would never want to be friends with someone like me…..I simply wasn't good enough for her! However, she had none of my hang ups and treated me much the same as she treated everyone else and by the time we both left the training establishment, a tenuous friendship had been formed.

Home again at the grand old age of nineteen I was jobless and at a loose end. My parents threw all sorts of ideas at me and eventually I accepted a job in Oxford, using my hotel training. At this stage I was coping a little better with life, but underneath, was still rather a lost soul. My predominant feeling was that of guilt, because I was harbouring a DREADFUL secret that could never be told. This made me very introverted and shy and I treated the men in my life really cruelly. In Oxford, I met and flirted with several young men in a very non-serious fashion until one day, when I was taken to a local night club, everyone was talking about the lead singer of the band which was playing that night. All my friends seemed to worship him and put a halo round his head, but I, as usual, saw nothing particularly special in him. However, I went along with the others to be introduced and afterwards, thought no more about it.

But word was whizzing around the town next day. The singer, apparently, was 'taken' with me and wanted to ask me out! Was I flattered? Of course I was, although

I had no intention of being anything other than the envy of the rest of Oxford. So, when the promised phone call came, I agreed to go out for a meal with him.

This man was different to anyone who had ever taken me out before. For a start he was eleven years older than me and was therefore beyond any of my usual tricks of 'lure, kick and let die'. He took me to one of the finest restaurants in Oxfordshire and treated me like a queen. I wasn't physically attracted to him, but he was certainly the kindest and most generous man who had crossed my path to date. We spent a very pleasant evening together, though I do remember feeling rather out of my depth because I knew absolutely nothing about his world of rock music.

So a friendship began which, from my point of view, was very tentative but my singer had fallen head over heals in love with me very quickly. Luckily, he was very patient with the young damaged girl that I was. Before long, a happiness started to envelope me that I had never known before. Here was a man who appeared to love me despite everything I had done and who accepted me for the sinner that I was! There were NO feelings of recrimination around him, nothing but love. He treated me to various days out, meals in country pubs, little gifts etc, and I lapped it up.

Then one day I took him to meet my parents and my bubble burst. He was not made to feel welcome in my parent's home. I was told he was not good enough for me. He wore rock singer clothes, had long, unruly hair, a common accent, high heels etc, etc, etc. Well......I could hardly take it all in. One of the kindest most generous and loving people I had ever met had just walked into my life and he wasn't GOOD enough? And from this moment on our friendship became a difficult affair. I continued to see him because we both lived in Oxford and I kept on thinking my parents would realise what a nice guy he was. But nothing of the sort happened. As our friendship developed, the concern of my parents deepened, until one day my father took it upon himself to write to my singer's mother, telling her that her son would never be acceptable to him as a son–in-law. What my father hoped to achieve by this I am not quite sure, but he certainly achieved a lot of hurt amongst the recipient's family.

Somehow, my singing friend and I continued an up and down friendship over the next few months and by the spring of 1977, we were talking about getting married. I was just twenty one and my singer was thirty two. When I told my parents that we were thinking about marrying, they declared that if we did, they would certainly not come to our wedding. However, all my friends were supporting the marriage proposals and wanted it to happen. I was beside myself with anxiety. That summer, I wrote several letters in a real state of anguish, though none were ever posted. I found them in my old writing case about three years ago and I quote two of them below, so that you can try and comprehend the turmoil of mind that I was in:

"Dear (Singer),

I've made a mess of everything. I don't want to muck you about any more. Please forget about me and find someone worthy of you. I'm very selfish but I know I can't take any more. Our worlds are different and I think we should keep in our own spheres. You have picked me out but I am far from ready for the depth of relationship that we have which is why the difficulties occur. I must grow up and know my own mind. Allow me, Please allow me, my youth............ "

The second letter which I feel I should share at this stage was written on the twenty third of July 1977, just two months before we got married.

"God didn't see fit to bless me with a seeing eye; he has left me to grope my way through life in blundering agony. I've tried so desperately to be like my mother but I'm a failure. Can't you see I'm a failure? I ought to shoot myself, not for my souls sake, but to stop the suffering of others, my dearest mother, but I'm cowardly and haven't the strength of my convictions. If I really felt it was the right way out I would do it, but something intangible tells me that my folly can be forgiven. Oh Lord, if there's any glimmer of hope show it to me now.... but don't you think it would be better to be out of harms way than to raise hopes and then create worse misery? Am I torn between the devil and the deep blue sea? I see only my mother's unhappiness and I cannot bear it. How can I rid myself of this bitterness, how can I find peace.......how can I regain my mothers trust? Why do I remain as a child, expecting to be forgiven as before? ......I am nobody, not anybody - I can't see why I was born, or am I as I feel – a human sacrifice!"

I should perhaps mention here that my family wasn't a particularly religious one. We attended church on Christmas day and sometimes at Easter and were taught to say a brief prayer as we got into bed when we were little. Other than that, most of my knowledge of religious type affairs was picked up from one or other of the many schools I attended......mostly, in fact, from a convent. Of all my senior schools, I was happiest at the convent. The headmistress was a nun and I was very fond of her. She taught us religious knowledge several times a week and brought the gospels alive in a very clever way. I thought at the time that most of her teaching had gone over the top of my head but looking back, I can see that she gave me a knowledge of the New Testament which was well above average.

In September 1977 my singer and I finally got married. It was a day that passed smoothly enough and which most of my relatives and friends remember with happiness, but for me it has never ever been a day I wish to recall. As we went through the traditional proceedings, my most over-riding thoughts were,

"Will mum and dad ever speak to me again? Have I lost my own family for ever? Have I done the right thing?"

I remember seeing my two sisters crying quietly in the corner of the room and knew that their sadness that our parents weren't present was deep. But to the world I looked happy and as we drove off on our honeymoon there was little reason for anyone to suspect what I was really thinking.

And so a marriage that was to last twenty eight years began. About three days after the wedding, while we were in Devon on our honeymoon, I remember walking passed a phone box and thinking,

"Dare I phone mum?"

I didn't stop at the time but the thought stayed with me. As more days went by I continued to think about it, until my agony of mind grew so much that I finally plucked up the courage to ring her, realising that I had to know, one way or the other, whether she was ever going to speak to me again. With my heart thumping noisily, I dialled and waited until I heard mum pick up the phone.

Then I said anxiously, "mum?"

She said, "Yes."

So I ventured, "Are you going to speak to me?" and she said yes again so I said,

"But I'm married, mum! I went ahead and did it"

She replied, "It doesn't mean I'm not going to speak to you."

And the conversation continued in a tentative manner until I finally realised all my fears were unfounded and although she hadn't come to the wedding, I was still her daughter and a relationship between us still existed. The relief was almost overwhelming and I do believe I enjoyed the rest of my honeymoon.

Over the following months, as I settled happily into married life, I began to calm down and my internal upset calmed with it. My husband was a very good man and although we had our ups and downs, generally he gave me the security and love I had been seeking. I was extremely fond of him and he really seemed to love me deeply and that compensated for many things. My parents, having made their stand, seemed to put it behind them and included my husband in the family circle, though my father really struggled to start with. As the next few years went by, my general feeling that I was such an awful person began to pale slowly into insignificance. The long road to recovery had commenced.

2

A Christian Experience

I HAVE ALWAYS THOUGHT IT possible that the things that were happening to me in my life would one day end up in a book, but I certainly didn't expect it to happen right now, just as I'm setting out on a new and very exciting venture. However, when I gave my life to God (or the universe or the greater power – whatever you choose to call it) many years ago, I gave it unconditionally and completely and the timing of these things is not decided by me so, having been guided to write a book now; that is what I shall do.

As I write, I am trying to recover from a very serious burst appendix which happened completely out of the blue, but which I can guarantee was part of the universal plan. As I lay in hospital, fighting unbelievable pain, my body struggling to respond to any pain killers in a beneficial way, I had completely decided that I would be happy to end this life. I was only extremely surprised that I was in this position at all because, before my appendix burst, I had sure I was about to serve on this earth in a very positive way. I certainly wasn't fighting a desire to live, because living in my body on this earth or, living without my body on this earth, hold very little difference for me, as I tend to spend my time somewhere between both worlds anyway. But as I lay on the hospital bed, being totally led and guided by 'source', certain things were shown to me that I could not ignore. I was told firmly that if I was to continue living this particular life, I had to stop hiding myself from the world and start living my truth openly. I was given quite a few examples of where I had been running away from the total truth and was shown how I half obey God's commands in many situations. Well, after I had been given some examples, I could not deny it was true and I felt very, very ashamed.

I lay in the darkness, thinking about all that had been revealed to me and I knew I was facing quite a choice. I must either stand in my truth and not be afraid to beam light wherever I was in the world, or continue as I had been, and probably die. I started to think hard about why I was so reluctant to stand up and be counted and to ask how I could possibly put it right. The answer came swiftly and at 3.30 am I called my husband (from whom I had been separated for two and a half years) and told him I was fighting for my life. Within an hour he was at my bedside holding my hand and listening as I gasped out my truth, as best I could...... and the process of my return to life began............

Just exactly when I first became conscious of 'the greater power' is impossible for me to pinpoint and I therefore suspect I was born with it. Certainly it was very natural to me to turn to God for help whenever I was in trouble and the first convent I attended very much encouraged this. It also encouraged turning to God when one wasn't in trouble, which I wasn't so keen on in those days! I had the most wonderful headmistress, (Sister Elizabeth) and she was a huge influence on the way I thought in my teenage years. She was a devout Christian woman and she told us many stories about Jesus that brought Him alive to us in a very understandable way. She also constantly incorporated His teachings into our every day lives, so there was never a doubt that He was very present in every situation, (in my mind, anyway!)

After I had committed the seemingly unforgivable sin of conceiving a baby and then 'killing' it, as I regarded it, I really felt it would be impossible for God to ever forgive me. I looked at churches askance and felt that I should never enter one again because of what I had done. My soul was in a very, very black space at that time and I had no communication of any kind that I was aware of, with a higher source.

But of course, unbeknownst to me, I was being very carefully looked after all the time and one day I found myself standing alone, outside an old Anglican church in Oxford. It may sound rather ridiculous but I honestly believed that if I went inside, heavy stones from the roof would fall on me. I looked up at it, imagined going inside, and immediately started trembling. I walked away and wandered around the nearby area for a while. But deep inside my little world of confusion I found myself being led back to the church, and I stood, gazing up at it once more. I felt my body go into a bit of a hot sweat as I thought,

"If I go in, the worst that can happen is that it will fall down on me."

I hovered and hovered, believing I was utterly despicable to even THINK that the church would welcome me after what I had done. But something deep inside me was pushing me to go in and find out. I crept up to the door and peeped in. There was no one around. I put my foot inside and stared up at the roof. Surely it would come down on me now! But nothing happened. I walked in a little way and stood in stunned silence. THE ROOF WAS NOT FALLING IN! I was standing in a church and the roof was NOT falling in. And my whole body was filled with awe and wonder. As I stood in the silence of that awesome moment, I committed my life to the service of God in a very, very deep way, vowing that if I could be forgiven for what I had done, I would forever be His servant. From that moment the hymn, '*Oh Jesus I have promised, to serve thee to the end.......*' became very meaningful to me.

It was not very long after this that I got married, (in a church!) and life started to change for me. One of my overriding problems with myself at this time was that when I was too scared to oppose my new husband or my parents, I would tell a lie. I hated myself for this weakness, and it really WAS a weakness, and as the years went by it got worse and worse. I'm not sure if anyone noticed it other than myself actually, but to me it seemed horrendous.

At about this time my husband and I moved to a small cottage in Herefordshire, situated on the banks of the river Wye. This was certainly a divinely inspired move, for we found ourselves in the most amazing little community of people, all with different social backgrounds and varying religious beliefs. Our cottage nestled in the midst of them all and whilst I quietly wrestled with my problem of honesty, I was bombarded on all sides by well meaning and wonderful neighbours, all older than myself and all keen to teach me about LIFE!

Over a number of years my husband and I became very close to the whole community. Half of them worshiped at the Welsh chapel and the other half at the local Anglican Church and they all seemed very keen to indoctrinate us into their systems. I was by now a young mum struggling to cope with my first child, making constant visits to all manner of doctors, trying to find out why my baby wasn't doing very well. It was a trying time but one which brought me ever closer to the local community. They all found time to visit me and offer their ideas of how I should go on. I felt immensely loved.

But, I distinctly remember long, troubled afternoons, walking the pram up and down the road, praying to God and saying,

"I know I'm this weak, horrible girl and I hate myself. Please, please can you come and take over my life and help me to be a better person?"

(I had by this time learnt from the chapel people about being 'born again') As the months and years went by I became more and more desperate in my pleas and increasingly certain that the only way to stop myself lying was by divine intervention. My whole person was becoming a one dimensional plea. I wanted nothing else than to experience this 'born again Christian experience' they all talked about. I was truly obsessed.

I suppose by the time my second child was born, my pleas had become fairly routine. I wanted to be born again just as much as ever but I didn't seem to be eligible to receive it! However, I still continued my walks along the road, often singing a song from the popular musical Godspell which seemed to epitomise what I longed for. *"Oh dear Lord, three things I pray. To see thee more clearly, love thee more dearly, follow thee nearly, day by day by day by day.........."* My prayers and song were a yearning from the bottom of my heart. But I was also caught up in the every day whirl of bringing up of two small children. We had discovered by this time that the eldest had a string of allergies which were affecting his development and the second, although she was very happy and healthy, brought all the difficulties of having two children and very little money.

By this time I had become quite friendly with a mum who lived about a mile away from our cottage. She had three children and was an ardent member of the chapel. She knew better than anyone else how much I desired to become a 'born again' Christian and she visited me frequently, trying to help. Through her more than anyone, I began to change my daily chant and pray in a more positive way. And finally my prayers were answered one momentous winter evening. I remember it was a very still, clear, starlit night and the children were fast asleep. My husband was working outside in the workshop and I decided to go upstairs in our tiny cottage and pray. I remember sitting on the bed and instead of praying I just stared into space. I began to talk to God as if He was sitting opposite me like a friend. I said,

"I have asked in every way I can think of, to die to myself and to become fully taken over by you and I don't know how to ask for it any more. I am so tired and I want you so much. Please show me if there is anything else I must do. Please will you take down the walls that appear to surround me and let me out of this prison. Help……help….. Please help!"

I sat in silence for a while, feeling the longing that I had with every bone and sinew in my body. Suddenly, I felt a huge surge of joy running through me and I knew something was happening! It seemed that the wall was being lifted and my body was being filled with heavenly light. Joy, light, joy, light! I knew with no shadow of doubt that my prayers were being answered and I was being …… born again!

Well, never, ever had I experienced such joy! I got up off the bed and raced downstairs. To my immense surprise the front door of the house stood wide open, despite the fact that it was a raw winter's night and I thought it had been firmly closed. I supposed it was a heavenly sign of some sort. I raced out to the workshop to see my husband and told him the news. He didn't have a clue what I was talking about but in my immeasurable joy I didn't care! I raced back into the house again and 'phoned up my friend. My joy was bursting out of me as I gabbled out the good news. She was delighted for me and when I told her about the door she said,

"I think you have a very special mission in life."

Then I rang my mum, wondering if she would understand. To my surprise, when I said to her,

"Mum! I've got there!" she replied,

"You mean you've started!"

I didn't question her response at the time, although I now realise what a wise statement it was. But at that moment I was too overjoyed to really hear her.

And so began what I call my 'Christian year' and it was probably one of the happiest years of my whole life. At this time my eldest son was between three and four years old and my daughter was a few months old, so life was pretty hectic for me. However, my new 'family' of Christian friends was everywhere. I was included in bible studies, chapel meetings, morning coffee groups etc and everyone it seemed, was anxious to know me. It was as if I had been welcomed into the most wonderful, enormous family I could ever imagine and the love I felt from them, and the love I felt for them, was quite amazing. My two children accompanied me everywhere I went and my life was unbelievably full and happy. Even my dad could see a difference in me.

But remember where I had been divinely placed! There were other elements at work amongst the communities that were around me and these comprised a Christian Scientist who lived two doors away from me, an atheist immediately next door and an avid church goer and Greenpeace fanatic on the other side. I loved all these neighbours dearly and they loved me, so the influences from the chapel were always being challenged!

The Greenpeace neighbour had a daughter some four years older than me, who happened to be living with her parents around this time, because she had a rare and complicated illness that needed constant nursing. I was getting to know her fairly well, but it wasn't possible to see her too often because she was rather weak. I was also a little wary, in case she was a fanatic like her mother, so I kept her at arms length and was content to visit her every now and then. However, over some Christmas festivities, I started to see a bit more of her and I began to realise that actually, we were very compatible. She wasn't at all like anybody else I had ever known and some of the things she said made a lot of sense to me. She must have liked what I was saying too because she used to call me her twin! One day, a truly enlightening day for me, she taught me a lesson that changed my life for ever and wrenched me out of the wonderful, peaceful, joyous, existence I had just found! It goes something like this:

I remember her standing opposite me in her driveway one evening and I was talking of rebirth and how one couldn't really know God unless one was born again. (This was very much the chapel way of thinking and I was well indoctrinated into it by now.) She looked at me intently and said,

"We are all equal in the sight of God, whether we are what you call 'born again' or not. I may not have had the experiences that you have had, but I have had my own experiences and they are no less and no more important than yours. There are many paths to heaven, not just the one that you and your chapel friends have taken and we are all a facet of it all".

I remember seeing her face clearly in the dark but I could hardly hear her words. I didn't WANT to hear her words. After all, wasn't I the happiest being on earth? Hadn't I FOUND what there was to be found? Hadn't God taken over my life in a momentous way, changed everything and made my existence bearable? Hadn't I been given the strength to stop lying? Didn't I belong to the only conceivable family? Why should I listen to what she was saying? And I vaguely heard her voice continuing………..

"I can see God in so and so and so and so. God is in me, and in my mum, and I can see God in you. I can see God everywhere, and in everyone!"…..and deep inside me something stirred and I felt very, very uncomfortable.

Later that night, when I was sitting in the bath, pondering vaguely about what she had said, I suddenly became aware that four faces were looking at me from various places in the bathroom! These four faces were of four very different people. One was President Gorbachev, who was actively the president of Russia at the time, one was myself, and there were two others, each from varying walks of life, whose identities I am unable to recall. But the important thing about my vision was that I could see God in each of these four very different people and the God shining out from them was equal in measure. I sat quite still, filled with amazement, becoming shockingly aware that my Christian beliefs had built a solid wall around my 'thinking' and I had shut out so much of the rest of the world in my joy of becoming a 'member' of the Christian family. In some measure, I had been judgemental. As the truth dawned deeper in me over the next few days, I felt ashamed for having been so narrow-minded. I likened my Christian experience to one of having lived in a huge balloon and I was part of the air inside the balloon. My friend, and my bath-time revelations from Source, had burst that balloon with an enormous bang, and I felt as if I was now floating in the rest of the air, lost and alone. A huge part of me felt incredibly sad, for I sensed that my days of unbelievable fellowship were about to come to an end but I also knew without a doubt, that it was time to move on. I felt very shocked that I had allowed such solid walls to surround me and I vowed never to let it happen again.

My daily thoughts changed quite dramatically after this, as one would expect. I didn't say anything to my Christian friends, but I started to realise there were differences between us. I began to see their walls, the same ones that I had had, that were built solidly around their Christian faith, and I felt a little frustrated with it. I still went to the prayer meetings however, and one day, I was sitting with my friends talking about baptism, and how various people had received real blessings after they had experienced a physical baptism. I inquired as to what was involved in a physical baptism and they explained that it meant a complete immersion in water. I thought to myself,

"I would like to receive a blessing like this."

All the way home I was thinking about baptism, and as soon as I got in my house, I went into the bathroom and filled the bath as full as it would go with water. It was pretty cold but I stripped off and plunged in! My four year old thought this was great fun and stripped off and plunged in with me! We shivered together and completely immersed ourselves in the water. I can't remember what I prayed at the time but whatever it was, it had a very powerful result.…………..

A few minutes later we were dressed again and sitting in the kitchen, warming ourselves in front of the rayburn. I casually reached out for my son and as I put my arms around him I felt an unnatural warmth coming from his tummy area. As we cuddled and talked about the bath, I pondered over this strong band of heat. I couldn't explain it but I knew it was something other than body heat. Later that day a Christian friend called to see me and I told her about the bath and the heat. I think she thought I was a little bit crazy to have immersed myself in the bath, and to my great disappointment she didn't comment much about the heat. When she left, I felt just as puzzled as before.

Later that day, whilst I was cooking supper, I heard a voice from seemingly nowhere saying,

"Your son has been healed."

I was very surprised! There was no-one in the room with me except my son, who was sitting on his potty in front of me – a habitual place for him as his allergies gave him so much diarrhoea. I returned thoughtfully to my cooking but it was not long before I heard the statement again! This time I knew it was inside my head. I took the supper off the oven, made sure than my son was safe and dashed upstairs where I huddled in a corner of my bedroom. Then began a conversation with 'source' that I will never ever forget. First I asked,

"Did you say my son has been healed?"

Immediately my heart swelled to about three times its normal size. It was a wonderful, glowing feeling. Then reason took over and I said,

"That's impossible!" And my heart immediately went small and it hurt. So I repeated,

"My son has been healed?" Again my heart swelled, just as it had the first time.

"But that's ridiculous" I said, and immediately my heart shrank.

As I huddled in the corner of the room I tested similar statements for at least ten minutes, always with the same result, until I gave it one final ultimatum:

"Are you really saying that my son has no more allergies. That he can eat just what he wants, whenever he wants, and that he is now as normal as any other child?"

Well I think I received the biggest glow of them all and it went on and on and on as I finally accepted the message, and was willing to believe it might be possible. After slowly picking myself up off the ground, I hesitantly went downstairs again. Well, what to do? I looked at my son and the pot of diarrhoea on the floor and finally I said to him,

"Would you like one of these pink wafers?"

"He looked at me uncertainly and said, "Will it be ok mum?"

I remembered the glow!

"Yes!" I replied and handed him one. I handed him a few other things he had never been able to eat before too, and he must have thought it was a very lucky day! He ate everything happily, looking trustingly up at me.

Whilst my son and I were enjoying this feast, my husband returned from work and I tried to tell him what had been going on. He thought I was an absolutely stark raving looney! He was extremely worried about the food that I was pumping down our son. But, lo and behold, there was NO diarrhoea! Even he had to admit that one minute our son was desperately allergic to various foods and the next he appeared to be able to eat anything. We were both quite dumbfounded really and as the days went by, and our son appeared to be as normal as any other boy, it became clear to me that he really had been healed!

Of course, living in such a close community as ours, the news of the healing soon spread around the village. I went up to the chapel the next Sunday, glowing with the wonder of it all and without really thinking about what I was doing, stood up in the middle of the service and told everyone about the healing. As I sat down again there was dead silence and then the next hymn was announced. I was a little bit puzzled by this and wondered why there had been no acknowledgement of my wonderful news! After the service my friend came up to me and I asked her why my news had been received so quietly. She carefully took me on one side and said,

"Women just don't speak in chapel, let alone stand up in the middle of a service like you did!"

I was incredulous!

"But this is such joyous news and a miracle that everyone should know about," I cried.

I couldn't believe that their chapel rules and regulations could stop everyone sharing the joy of the moment and that the Glory of God should not be revelled in at this very special time. But so it was, and of course with it came a great change in my attitude towards these lovely and well-meaning chapel people.

The other thing to note at this time was a little incident that occurred about two months later. It took place when I had taken the children for a walk and we dropped in to see an old couple who lived just outside the village. As we sat having a cup of tea, they were talking about healing and about the heat which often accompanies healing. Well after that I hardly heard another word because it was in that moment I realised that my son had actually been healed when I had felt the heat around his body after the baptism. As I was ignorant of this at the time, the Holy Spirit had had to find another way to awaken me to the healing that had taken place. Hence the bedroom scenario! I also realised that a great healing gift had been given to me after the baptism and my son had also received an enormous blessing that would change his life forever, although he was completely unaware of anything at the time. I did, later, question the friend who had called on me that day and asked her why she had not explained what had happened to me and she replied very wisely,

"I knew you had to find out for yourself."

And of course she was absolutely right, because from that exceptionally momentous day to this, the Holy Spirit uses the very same means of communication that it so painstakingly taught me to recognise and trust, whilst I was huddled in the corner of the bedroom.

3

Going beyond the Boundaries and unearthing a past life

As I waded my way through the next few months, I was to see a far bigger picture of life and religion than I had previously begun to dream of. The shock of being catapulted out of the 'Christian label' was such that I vowed never to allow walls to block my spiritual growth again if I could help it. I was quite ashamed at how small-minded I had been as a born-again Christian, and I realised there would be many other traps to fall into along the path of life. I prayed hard that I should be kept clear of them and thus I began a new phase of my life as a seriously 'unlabelled' being.

The shifts that took place after my bathroom baptism slowly put a gap between myself and my friends. I didn't say too much to them, because I loved them all dearly and I didn't really know how to explain how I felt. But when we moved to a bigger house about five miles away and my third child was born, it created a natural 'distancing' from them.

My third child, Edward, was my second son, and it seemed to me that there was a huge depth of attachment between us straight away. What I did find quite unnerving was the fact that from the moment Edward was born, I kept feeling we weren't going to be together for very long. I didn't know why I should be feeling like this. Also, from the first, he never seemed to sleep the night through. He would wake up screaming and I knew he was having nightmares. Every single time I had to get out of bed, cuddle him for a while and then he would fall back to sleep again. This became such a routine that I got completely used to it until he grew older and started to say things like,

"Mummy, Mummy, I thought you were dying!"

I used to reassure him as best I could but it was quite upsetting for us both.

At around this time I became aware of the concept of reincarnation. It wasn't a subject I had thought about much at all, but one evening, on happening to watch a television programme about a reincarnated child, I knew with tremendous inner certainty that I had lived before. Beginning to talk about it to my mother and I told her I thought I had been a witch in France and I had been burnt at the stake. I was expecting a massive rebuff but she simply said,

"Well that would explain why you speak French with such a natural accent!"

From my mother this was amazing indeed! So she

thought I could have lived before! I asked her if she thought she had lived before and she said,

"I have been told that I have!"

I think most of my amazement came from the fact that my mother had never talked about reincarnation to me, so I naturally assumed that it wasn't part of her beliefs.

After that I started to think seriously about my previous life and gradually became aware of which region in France it had happened, and also that I had lived in an oldish house in the middle of some woods. I had been a healer of some sort and had been a good one. I knew I had been put to death because healers had been so little understood in those days, and not because I had been a bad person in any way.

The next few years passed peacefully enough, with the children taking up most of my time and school timetables dominating our daily routine. I had formed a new set of friends who were quite different from any of my previous ones, and the only contact I had with anything church-like was the Sunday school.

Then came yet another momentous day. It was a Saturday and all the family were at home. The children, by then aged ten, seven and five, were out in the garden with my husband, lighting a bonfire and I was on my own in the kitchen, cooking the lunch. Suddenly, my five year old came racing down the garden screaming,

"Mummy, Mummy," at the top of his voice.

The kitchen door burst open and he flung himself into my arms.

"Mummy, I thought you were burning!" he sobbed.

As I held Edward tightly in my arms I knew in an instant, that he had either seen me burn in the previous life or he had known of it. Somehow the bonfire in the garden must have sparked a memory for him and he had relived the terror of an unforgettable moment. He was racked with sobs and it took a long time to calm him down. As we hugged closely together, I knew he had been my son before and this experience served to confirm all I had previously suspected about myself and my life as a witch. The shock was absolutely enormous, but it did help to explain Edward's constant nightmares and why I had always felt that he and I would be separated.

This very defining moment in my life had one huge effect on me. It now became an absolute necessity for me to open up my thinking and try to unravel this past life, because there could be no disputing that it had happened and it was affecting my son. I decided it was time to investigate reincarnation as best I could. I asked fervently for God's help!

It dawned on me that there may be a pattern to what was happening in our present lives and that my son and I had reincarnated together in this life in order to heal the hurts of the previous life. I started to tell him we had come together in this life to BE together and that I knew we would always be together. He trusted me and on the nightmare nights I was gradually able to calm him a little bit quicker each time. I couldn't turn to any of my Christian friends at this time because reincarnation simply wasn't in their belief system. So I started to speak to other people, in fact anyone and everyone. Books turned up which helped me and my mother turned out to be very open minded about these things. Though never volunteering much herself, she was happy to listen to my wandering thoughts.

I remember vividly one day going to see Sally, a healer who was visiting the area. I had never met another healer before and as I was shown into her room, got the fright of my life. Sally, looked exactly how I imagined a witch would look, with long grey hair sticking out from her head! She sat cross legged on a cushion in front of me and though frightened, I tried hard not to show it! She was able to tell me that my youngest son had not witnessed my death although he had been at the house when I was taken away by the soldiers. Edward had been very, very frightened and feeling extremely powerless as it happened. He had remained hiding in the house for many days afterwards, too scared to go out. I asked Sally if she could help him to get rid of the nightmares. She said she could and she also told me many things about myself and my family which I didn't understand at the time. Luckily she made a tape of the session which I listened to and appreciated, some fifteen years or so later!

A few days after I saw Sally, Edward was having another of his nightmares so I climbed into his bed, held him very firmly, and said to him,

"Darling, mummy is not going to die in this life! I did die and leave you in a previous life but we have come together in this life to put it right. This life we are going to BE together."

I let him think about this for a few minutes and then told him not to be fearful of what had already happened because it was history, it was over, and the whole of our future was before us. And I am pleased to say, this was the last nightmare he ever had!

Having now asked to open up my mind to accept all sorts of new concepts, I began to benefit from communication with my maternal grandmother who had died when I was three years old. Obviously I hadn't known her very well in the physical although I could remember a few times when I had stayed with her. I was digging in the garden one day when I first became aware of her presence. After a while she started speaking to me. I was incredulous at first, thinking I must be going mad, having an in depth conversation with someone in my head. And yet the conversation was very real and very exciting! It came in exactly the same way as the communication I had had in the kitchen when the universe was trying to tell me that my elder son had been healed. The only person I mentioned it to was my mother who seemed very pleased and said she wished she could speak to her. This matter of fact response encouraged me to continue my conversations and over the coming months, a very strong line of communication was formed. I became enormously attached to my grandmother and learnt many things from her. Also, at about this time, various people turned up for healing and, although I rarely told anyone what had happened to my eldest son, a few people recognised the gift in me and came for help.

One person who came to me for help was a newcomer to the village in which I now lived. I will tell her story here as it serves to show how the universe was teaching me to use the gifts that I was gradually acquiring. She had a daughter who was slightly older then my eldest son and they were in the same class at school. However, our real connection was our faith in God and we met regularly with the children at Sunday school. We began to spend time together and talk about our spiritual lives in a trusting way. I knew she desperately wanted another child and, as I had three, I sympathised with her greatly. Then one day I met her in the street and remember saying to her, apparently completely randomly,

"Its time for you to conceive your second child!"

She simply looked at me, then agreed, and nothing else was said. As I walked away I thought to myself:

"I am an absolute nutcase. Whatever made me say that to her!!"

And yet I knew in my heart that it was right.

Two months later, this friend and I met in the waiting room at the doctor's surgery. She told me she was going to see the doctor because she thought she was losing the baby she was carrying. I was incredulous for I knew that this baby was divinely inspired and this shouldn't be happening. A few minutes later she was called in to see the doctor, but not before I had arranged to go and see her that afternoon.

In a very anxious state of mind, I visited my new friend. She told me that the doctor thought she had lost the baby and would need to go into hospital for a D and C(a scraping of her womb). I felt everything inside me screaming opposition to this decision and wondered whether to tell her. Instead, I asked if I could possibly put my hand over her stomach. She said she felt the baby was dead but didn't mind me trying. What followed was quite amazing. As we sat in the cosy confines of her kitchen, I, with my left hand just above her womb, we didn't say a thing to each other and were quite calm in the silence. Gradually, we both felt a stirring of energy, as if something in her stomach was coming to life. I felt certain that her baby was alive and told her. She looked me straight in the eye and said I could be right! We sat there a little longer, trying to take in what was happening. I then hesitantly asked,

"Are you willing to challenge the doctor when you go into hospital and tell him you think the baby might be alive?"

Sensibly, she replied that she would ask for a scan.

There followed a very anxious few days while she was taken into hospital for her supposed D and C. She asked for a scan, telling the medics she felt the baby might be alive. Lo and behold, as soon as she was connected to the scanning machine, it showed a little heart beat! Oh Joy! She was kept in hospital for a few days, just for monitoring, and as soon as she was discharged, I went straight round to see her. We both knew a miracle had taken place and we both knew for certain that the baby would be perfectly alright. It was a marvellous moment indeed but one we never shared with anyone outside our own families. She said the time was not right for my gift to be common knowledge, and although I was disappointed at the time, looking back, she was probably right.

The importance of this story is that it highlights the beginning stages of the universe's methods of working through me, both by deep inner knowings showing themselves in a very calm and natural way and through the use of my left hand, my healing hand. No song and dance accompanied what happened and these were very much the hallmarks of my early healings.

You may well be wondering why I mention the use of my left hand for healing rather than my right. Indeed it is a strange story and one that I feel may have more to unfold. Shortly after my baptismal bath, when the father of an old Christian friend of mine became very ill with cancer. I visited him in hospital and he told me that the doctors were going to remove his left arm, just above the elbow. He had tremendous faith in God and when it became clear he would have to lose his arm he simply dedicated what was going to happen to 'The Lord' announcing bravely:

"If He doesn't want me to have my arm, then so be it."

A few days later, his arm was removed. He remained in hospital because the cancer had spread to other areas of his body and his future health was very uncertain. I can remember the huge concern of his family at this stage but was not closely involved with what happened to him next. Very importantly though, as I was learning to receive messages from the 'other world', one that came clearly through at this time was: 'AND HIS MIGHTY ARM WILL REPLACE YOURS IN SUCH A WAY THAT YOU WILL GLORIFY HIS NAME FOR EVER!' I knew this referred to my friend's father, so I wrote it down and sent it to him at the hospital, via my friend. I didn't know what it meant but it had a hopeful feel to it so I thought it might help! A few days later he died.

Shortly after this old man's death, I started to have the strangest pain in my left arm just above the elbow and soon realised that this was where his arm had been cut off. I then got a feeling of numbness in my left hand and it was strange to touch, almost as if there was an invisible layer between my hand and anything it encountered. It often tingled strongly, a tingling which reached right to the cut off point above the elbow. Gradually I began to realise that because this very Christian man had given his arm to God with total trust and unconditional love, somehow I was the chosen recipient of his gift and in future my arm would be used for great healings. It was very strange indeed!

There is definitely a close link between my friend's father and myself and to this day I am often aware of his presence around me. He actually confirmed his presence shortly after his death by appearing to me in the supermarket while I was shopping. I was going along an aisle with my trolley, my mind totally pre-occupied with what I was going to buy, when, suddenly I saw him ahead. I stopped dead in my tracks and he gave me the most wonderful smile. I was so surprised that I must have looked away for a minute and when I looked back again, he had disappeared! The face now in front of me was that of the man who really owned the body. Somehow my friend's father had superimposed himself on this stranger's face to reveal himself to me and I felt an incredible sense of happiness surge through me. I did not try to tell my friend of these happenings. By that time I was drawing away from her somewhat and in any case, wasn't sure that I understood completely what was happening myself! I just knew it WAS happening, and as I said at the beginning of this particular story, I feel there may be more to be revealed, in its own good time.

And so it is that, if I need to use a hand for healing purposes, I always use the left one. There is usually a distinct difference between how my two hands feel but I have grown so used to this that I now rarely think about it. If I were to attempt a reason for this being so, it would be that the difference between them serves as a constant reminder of what I am able to do with one hand and am not able to do with the other!

One other incident which turned out to have great future value involved a visit to another mum I vaguely knew in my village. For some while she had struggled with severe back problems and had been bed ridden for the last few months. I turned up on her doorstep one day, (I can't for the life of me remember why), and I don't think she was very pleased to see me. She didn't know me very well and had quite enough to cope with. However, she put aside her own problems and politely invited me in for a cup of coffee. During the course of conversation I said to her,

"Would you like to see if there's any healing available for you?"

She was very, very sceptical but there was another friend in the room with us and I rather think this swayed her to say a hesitant,

"Yes."

I put my hand behind her and felt the usual heat and energy. I left it behind her, giving it time to do whatever was needed, then I quickly finished my coffee and left, feeling rather uncomfortable and wondering if I had done the right thing. What I didn't know was that this mum, who I shall call Hannah, had had a terrific reaction to my healing hand! She felt heat run up the centre of her back when my hand was behind her but because it had all been so unexpected, hadn't known what to say. Apparently she had started to feel easier in her back the minute I left the house. But the first thing I knew of it was when she 'phoned me the next day to say she was running up and down the road and wanted to know how on earth this had happened. I was overjoyed, not just for her but for myself too. I had experienced very few instant healings at this stage and it did an enormous amount for my self-confidence. As far as Hannah was concerned, it changed her life for ever. From being the greatest cynic she suddenly began looking into the 'spiritual' realm with much eagerness and has continued to do so with great results for the last twenty years. Watching Hannah's early progress also made me aware, in no uncertain terms, that mine was no ordinary gift of healing because WHEN a healing occurs through me, it is a life changing experience for the recipient. I began to realise that I was able to facilitate a very deep type of healing which could get to the true root of people's problems.

And so my spiritual education continued...........

4

Confusion and a big move

Here I am, standing here, loving you,
Wanting you to work your will through me,
Knowing somehow I must be blocking you,
But knowing there's nothing I can do.

I'm feeling rather trapped inside my body,
I want to show the world how much you care,
But I really don't know which way I am turning,
And I have to wait for you before I share,

Oh! Why am I so bad at waiting for you,
But I know its best for me that I should rest,
Please fill me up with patience and with knowledge,
For that's the way that you can use me best.

4/12/88

MY STATE OF MIND OVER the next few years was very
rocky. I was, to the outside world, busy with bringing
up my three children. I was desperate to do it to the
best of my ability so my days were long and very full.
All three children were very good tennis players and we

spent many happy hours at tennis tournaments with our friends. But deep in my core, although there were times when I felt extremely at peace, there were other times when I felt completely lost and alone, wondering where it was all leading. I always knew that I wanted to be used by the universe to the fullest extent possible but it seemed that very little that I set out to do ever really flourished. Yet at the same time, huge revelations were occurring and I was growing steadily in my knowledge of spiritual matters and life itself. I was doing occasional healings but predominantly, during those years, I was broadening my outlook in other ways; reaching into every corner that I could for my own personal growth.

I often tried to put my feelings into words and one day I remember writing the following, from the depths of my heart:

'Life is a long, lonely journey with hard, hard lessons to be learnt. I search constantly for peace, love, true freedom, true righteousness. I feel lost, but I am not lost. I am loved, though I cannot always feel it. I search for good and only good on this mixed up planet. I search for a true roll to fulfil in this life and I long for eternal peace when I am done. I have a constant yearning to help others and I long to be actively bringing truth and ultimately healing to sufferers. I yearn for more knowledge of the deceased and for more communication with all types of the deceased. I long to be a better and freer person so that I may be used as much as possible to bring the meaning of truth and life to all that I can. But for now, I feel that I can only wait.'

I kept up my search for matters concerning reincarnation and occasionally became aware of new snippets belonging to my life as a witch. I knew, for instance, that my mother in that life was the same mother that I had in this life. She had been totally unable to cope with what I was doing, three hundred and fifty years ago, mainly because she didn't understand the sort of things that I did and was embarrassed by me. I knew that my daughter in this life had been my sister in that life and that she had thought very much as my mother had. She had felt almost glad that I had been put to death because I was so much trouble to the family. I could even sense her mocking me as I died. These revelations helped to explain some of my mother's attitude towards spiritual matters in this life and also the ongoing difficult relationship that I had with my daughter. I began to wonder who else had been involved in that past life and why we were altogether again in this life. And as my wonderings started to take shape, more and more was revealed to me......

However, in September 1996 my father died rather unexpectedly and this brought about huge changes to myself and my family. We were living in rural Herefordshire at the time, but we had been trying to move to Monmouthshire for the last two years because the children were all at school there. However, for some reason, we had been unable to sell our house and also had not been able to find anywhere suitable to move to. Little did I know at the time that nothing was working out because the universe had other plans for us, but all was revealed to me two days after my father's death, when I received an unexpected inner message. I was walking down the lawn in our Herefordshire property when I distinctly heard dad's voice saying to me,

"Go and look after mum."

I was really very surprised, because it was not something I had ever considered, but now that dad had mentioned it to me, it did make complete and utter sense. I continued down the lawn, my mind racing!

Moving a husband and three children in a completely different direction to the one in which we were expecting to go, would take a huge amount of reorganisation, but as if the universe wished to confirm this was exactly the right thing to do, we received an offer on our Herefordshire property almost at once. At the same time, my mother was telling the family she wanted to remain on the farm and she would manage it on her own, somehow! This was very worrying for us because she was seventy one and had a heart complaint that was fairly tricky to cope with. I suggested to my sisters that I and my family might be interested in moving to the farm. I had realised that in one years' time, each of the children would be at a suitable place in their education to move schools. My husband had been telling me for some time that he wanted to retire and there were a few voluntary redundancies on offer. Besides, he was absolutely bowled over at the thought of farming for a living. I myself was tired of my career and would welcome a change and most of all we would all absolutely love to live with my mum. But I did have a very definite feeling of reservation about living back at my old home, and I wasn't sure why. The more I thought about it, the more I told myself that I mustn't be selfish, for the move would certainly suit the rest of the family. We did vaguely consider leaving mum on her own on the farm and simply moving to a property of our own close by, to keep an eye on her, but it seemed totally impractical in view of the fact she was far too old to manage the farm single-handedly and we would be forever on the road between our house and hers, trying to help her.

So, one year later, we found ourselves packing up everything; our home, our jobs, the schools, our friends and starting out on a completely new venture. Our house had sold very easily to a different buyer, (we had lost the first one by this time) my husband applied for and got his voluntary redundancy, and we had found three good new schools for the children. My mother had meanwhile decided that she would move out of the farmhouse and convert one of the outbuildings into living accommodation for herself. She wanted us to have the main house on our own and she was ready for something smaller anyway. This proved to be an absolutely marvellous idea because she, and we, had the best of both worlds; our privacy, and yet the security of knowing each other were nearby.

I had absolutely no idea how much the move was going to change the spiritual side of our lives but I suppose, looking back, it was a bit like the cork coming out of a champagne bottle. It happened initially because of the major physical changes that naturally occur with a house move. Then, living so close to my mother meant that her and my relationship needed to become completely harmonious and that took many months to work out. Also, my husband and I were living, sleeping, eating and generally 'being', in the same space all day long and the intensity of this proximity brought up huge difficulties that had to be addressed. As far as the children were concerned, they were now living much closer to their grandmother and she had a huge influence on their lives and also the farm itself had an immensely powerful energy that was to accelerate all of us along our paths as spiritual people. We started to deal with issues hitherto unknown to us, both from this life and from past lives. Before we had been there long, however, it became totally clear to me that we had always been destined to move to the farm and we were simply marking time during the two years that our previous house was on the market and we had been property hunting. This served to show me yet again how LARGE the divine plan is and how SMALL we are in it!

5

Hearing and then learning to trust the great inner voice

DON'T IMAGINE A HUGE STRING of changes occurred straight away! The universal plan is far more intricate than humans can ever possibly hope to understand and many wrong paths were taken before the right ones were found. I have related things as they come to mind, trusting that they will be revealed in the correct order!

We settled into farm life fairly easily. The children loved the countryside and as they were still keen tennis players, living in Gloucestershire made travelling to the tournaments much easier than from Herefordshire and less time was spent on the road than before. My husband had never had anything to do with farming before but he flourished under mum's guidance and was incredibly happy starting out on his new career. He had decided to breed rare sheep and set about the task with real enthusiasm and a pile of books from the library! I was very happy to live such an outdoor active life and started to enjoy flower gardening for the first time and walking the dogs.

I suppose the change in our circumstances hit myself and my youngest son Edward hardest, at the beginning. Although I was very, very pleased to be taking care of my mum, and loving the freedom of the farm life, there was a constant feeling of unease inside me which was uncomfortable to live with. I had no idea why this should be and as I was very busy with school runs and all the complications that three children starting three new schools brought, I didn't have too much time to think about it. But Edward, our happy go lucky eleven year old, failed to settle into his new school and from the very first day, said he didn't think it was the right place for him. He never wanted to get out of the car in the mornings when we arrived, and he was getting more and more tearful about going to school at all, as the weeks went by. After a couple of terms I actually became unable to force him into school because he was so distressed and I had to keep him at home. I decided that the high powered school he was at was probably unsuitable for him because, although the teachers there claimed to understand dyslexia, (Edward was dyslexic), I don't think they realised just how many other areas of a child's life it affected, besides reading. So many teachers thought that dyslexic children were idiots, and treated them as such in front of the other children, thus undermining their confidence in every area of school life. Edward had a very low opinion of himself. He knew he was not as competent as other children and felt different because had to go for special lessons and this 'difference' subsequently showed up in most of his other school activities. He was also struggling with the general behaviour of his compatriots, he being of a very gentle, loving nature, and finding the bullying tactics of his class mates extremely distressing.

My daughter at the time was going to a different school, which we weren't altogether happy with, but we decided that it would help Edward enormously if he could attend the same school as her and have her around to support him during the school day. She felt very maternal towards him, and took great care of him, certainly helping him over the hurdle of getting back into education. But it was a rushed decision, not necessarily the right one, and all of this served to increase my overall feeling of unease.

Over the next few years we certainly had our fair share of problems with our children and most of this taught me, and them, invaluable lessons about life. It also opened up a new type of relationship with my mother and restarted a trusting dialogue between us that had been absent for a very long time. She was incredibly helpful over all our trials and tribulations, using her own life's lessons to advise us, with a wisdom that only age can bring.

I had a very strong desire at this time, to make my mother's life as happy as I possibly could and that I should not fail to put her best interests at the top of my agenda, whenever possible. Therefore, whatever she wanted to do on the farm was hers for the asking. Whatever she needed, I gave her. In fact I gave my ALL for her comfort and pleasure, making things harder for myself, if necessary. Then one day, not long before she died, I asked her if what I was doing was making up for the dreadful things I had done as a teenager. She said it was. I asked her if I could be forgiven for what I had done and if the slate could be wiped clean now and my relief was unparalleled when she said,

"Yes definitely." I knew very little about karma at this stage but I now realise that my strong desire to give her my all was prompted by my need to make reparations for misdeeds earlier in my life and I vowed to continue this until her dying day. I was overwhelmed with relief that at last I could be forgiven for what I had frequently referred to as my 'Black sheep' days and I never, ever wanted to fail my mother again.

Meanwhile, my growing closeness to my mother was highlighting problems that I had with my husband. If you remember back to the first chapter, I had originally married him because I found in him the love and security that I had failed to find from my parents all those years ago. So it stood to reason that as my relationship with my mother healed, the relationship with my husband became less necessary and the gaps between us started to show. This was made worse by the fact that we were living in each others pockets all the time and it seemed to me as if I could never get away from him. While he had been employed by a third party, he had been out of the house all day and this had given me enough freedom to do what I wanted to do. But a self-employed farming life is very different and I was gradually becoming choked by my lack of private time. I was also becoming aware that while he had been employed, he had been constantly motivated by someone else, but now he was working for himself he needed motivating and supporting by me and I found this very draining. Eventually, I was becoming so fatigued by it all, that I started to take the car out and park in a quiet spot somewhere, in order to escape into my own world.

The feelings I have just recounted had been creeping up on me slowly; there was no sudden start to it all. And as slowly as it happened, the past life that I had been made aware of began to take a much larger part in my thoughts. I had started talking to Edward about spiritual matters on a fairly regular basis and he seemed to understand everything and take it all in his stride. In fact, when he was staying in a hotel with me one night I could hardly stop him talking and he remarked,

"I love talking about these things!"

He was eleven years old at the time!

My mother was a bit anxious about the content of our conversations but even she could see that Edward had a very special understanding and was wise beyond his years. And over the next few years, through many discussions, the previous life which we had shared started to become clearer to us both and he began to understand why he was struggling in certain areas of this life. There was a momentous day when I decided to share with him that I thought his father had been the soldier responsible for putting me to death on the bonfire. I told him that I didn't think his father had known me personally, but he had carried out the deed because it was his job. He had, at that time, a very low opinion of witches and thought the world was well rid of them when they were put to death. But somewhere, in the act of killing me, something had happened and I felt that his father had become aware that I was a good woman and that he had made a mistake.......... I then waited with baited breath to see how my son would react to my words and was amazed when, after a short pause, he simply said,

"Well, that feels about right!"

I went on to tell my son that I thought that his father and I were somehow together in this life because he was searching for the truth.

Over the coming months the conviction that my husband had put me to death grew stronger and stronger. I also started to realise that most of the people around me in this life were the same people that were around me in that last life and we had all reincarnated together for a reason. As Edward and I spoke to each other more, we discovered that the experiences he was having in this life were bringing up emotions he had previously experienced in the past life. They were showing themselves in order to bring about healing because once the past life was healed he wouldn't need to experience the emotions again in this life. A whole new meaning to his difficulties at school started to unfold. It was around this time that he suffered some serious bullying and had been found by a teacher at one stage, sitting on the loo, wondering how best to end it all. The teachers were marvellous and knew how to put an immediate stop to the bullying. He was then monitored carefully at school and given total unconditional love and support by me, which was something I had failed to do in the past life.

Around this time I was taken into a deep trance state by the Holy Spirit, where I experienced the feelings that Edward had experienced as I was put to death. I was shifted from one level of consciousness to another and as it encompassed me I could feel my son's distress. I knew that as I had died, he felt totally betrayed by me. I had knowingly put myself in danger of my life when I became a healer, and had no thought of the consequences that my death would have on him or anyone else in the family. He had loved me in a totally trusting and unconditional way in that life and the shock of my death was overwhelming to his system. After my death he had felt very vulnerable, almost as if he was guilty of something himself and he hid himself away from the world, because he was so scared. As the spirit world made me relive his feelings, I knew he had never managed to overcome the intense grief and feeling of betrayal that my death had brought on him and he had lived the rest of that life in a very dark place.

My son and I were incredibly close at this time and it never occurred to us to doubt any of the things that were being revealed. In fact, the whole episode that had been revealed to me under the spiritual influence I have just related made so much sense to my son that he began to understand himself and his feelings in this life very much better. He realised that he was allowing himself to be a victim of bullying in this life because he was reliving the feeling of being a victim in the past life. We started to talk to each other very deeply about how this could be put right and I remember humbly asking if he could possibly forgive me for not looking after him properly in our last life and allowing my 'profession' to have complete control of how I behaved. I told him I now knew how wrongly I had treated him and how I was doing everything that I could in this life to put it right. He already knew this and forgave me whole heartedly! Immediately we felt a huge weight lift from our shoulders. But this was only the tip of the iceberg and over the next few years I had many, many trance states and our lives were a continual unravelling of the damage that had been done to him in the past and how we could put it right. My son was as eager as I was because each revelation helped to heal his path in this life and he started to become a stronger and more balanced person.

As Edward got older, quite a lot of our revelations started to come through his tennis. We would go down to the tennis court together, seemingly to have a training session, but time after time it would turn out to be a spiritual lesson for us both. I would be feeding balls to him from a basket and he would start to complain that he didn't feel right about himself. He would then start to hit the tennis balls all over the place and get very frustrated! I would then take a look at his aura and pick up whatever the universe was showing us for the day. We would talk it over until the problem was unravelled. As soon as we learnt the lesson we were supposed to learn, I would go back to feeding the balls from the basket and he would start to hit them back in an amazing fashion and all was right with our world. Over time, I learnt to be incredibly quick at picking up what he needed to know and this has turned out to be a massive asset in my healing abilities. I didn't realise what was happening at the time but I now know I was learning to read his aura in perfect detail and I can now read anyone's aura in the same precise way.

And then came the day that the universe began to turn things around and I was encouraged to back off and let Edward pick up the lessons for himself. I was still feeding tennis balls to him but I took on a very different role when things went wrong. I became more like a guide. We still continued to have reference to the past life in these sessions and on one particular, crucial day he realised he had the following choice: he could either go on living under the cloud that he had lived in after my death (which was what he was familiar with) or he could put it behind him and move out from the cloud, knowing now, I would never ever do it to him again. We both knew this was a very important part of his healing and we had come together in this life especially to put this right and I had certainly left no stone unturned to do exactly that. He gradually realised he had nothing to fear and he could live safely and happily in the future. The love and security that I was showering on him were gently healing him.

It should be noted here that on the face of it, I was doing nothing that any other ordinary loving parent wouldn't do in trying to help their child; in fact it is being done all over the world all the time. The difference for us was that we knew WHY it was all happening and how our current situation was totally linked to what had happened several centuries before!

6

Putting the knowledge of the past life into healing this life

ALTHOUGH WHAT WAS BEING REVEALED to my son and I during these years was very consuming, there were many other things going on at the same time. My daughter was having her fair share of problems and unfortunately she and I did not have the best of relationships so it was quite difficult for us to cope with them. At the age of thirteen she was playing tennis at the highest national level for her age and she was very happily being transported around the country to various tennis tournaments by her father. I think the problems started, partly from the school she was attending, where she was made to feel an oddity because she spent so much time away playing tennis and partly from her own natural process of growing up and beginning to assess who she was. By the time she was fourteen she was starting to look for excuses not to play tennis and to find fault with her father who was accompanying her. Suddenly, one day, she announced that she wasn't going to play any more. I was very happy about this because I had never felt she was really cut out for the tennis professional's life but her father was devastated. He had put a lot of time and effort into helping her and he couldn't come to terms with her sudden decision. A rift began between them and she started to blame him for all sorts of things and to turn for comfort to young men in her class who had hitherto gone unnoticed.

My daughter then went through a couple of unmanageable years, going from boyfriend to boyfriend and eventually getting herself so tied up in knots that she eventually attempted to take her own life. I know there are a lot of 'cries for help' amongst sixteen year olds that often end up in overdoses but I was around at the time that it happened and I do know that my daughter really was at the end of her tether and desperately wanted to end it all. One day, she ate every single pill that was in the cupboard in our bathroom in less than five minutes. It was very lucky that I found her within minutes of doing this and was able to rush her straight into the local hospital. After a long and difficult night in one of the wards, she was allowed home and we began the long road of trying to come to terms with what she had done. This dreadful event was the start of a huge change in her and the relationship between her and I began to change too. I, for one, had nearly lost my daughter, and she had been saved by a mum whom she had hardly wanted to KNOW before!!

And so began a time of re-evaluation for us all. Also at around this time I began to realise that my daughter had a part in that fateful past life that probably needed healing! I already knew she had been my sister and completely unsympathetic to my cause. I now became aware that she had probably been near the scene when I had been put to death and she had been glad of what was happening because I was an embarrassment to her amongst her associates and friends. I was then reminded of the link between my daughter and my husband in this life and suddenly I suspected that it came from a recognition of being 'partners in crime' from the past life. I don't think she actively knew my husband in that life but she had definitely picked up the underlying rapport that lay at the deeper level, in this one. Also she had an incredibly close relationship with my mother and I knew she was feeling the attachment from the past life.

The next year my daughter changed schools because we didn't dare leave her at the one where she was having so much trouble. The next school had a much stricter regime but from day one she was extremely happy, so she decided she would like to become a boarder. This meant I had much less contact with her but that didn't stop me asking God continually for our relationship to be healed. Her relationship with her father was diabolical by now but as mine was disintegrating with him too, we found a certain amount of solace in each other. I never set out to tell her anything in particular but she had an incredible knack of wheedling things out of me because she seemed to already be aware of the problems I was having. All I knew was, since her attempt on her life, I wanted to be really close to her, and I was desperately asking the universe to heal the past life, without having a clue how it could be accomplished.

One day, when I was busy doing some housework, I was taken into one of my 'altered states' and suddenly I was aware of being at the site of the bonfire and my daughter was there. She was standing watching all that was going on. I felt almost as if she was jeering at me. And as I watched, I was made aware of my daughter's inner realms and I saw that there was a part of her that wanted to be forgiven. She had come into this life to draw attention to her relationship with me and to see if there could be any reconciliation between us. There and then, from on top of the bonfire, I held out my hands towards her and cried,

"I forgive you. I love you! Please forgive me for not considering YOUR feelings more as a sister and hurting you. I did not mean my family to get hurt by what I was doing. I truly believed I was acting for the highest good and that my family should accept this. Now I realise I was wrong and I am truly sorry. I should have been more thoughtful. I forgive you for jeering at me and for feeling all the things that you felt."

And I felt as if we moved towards each other right there, at the scene of the bonfire and at this deep level we hugged each other unconditionally.

That very night, at midnight, I received a telephone call from my daughter. She was phoning from school saying she was sick and could she come home. I hesitated for a moment and then replied that I thought the school would look after her. To my horror she then told me that she wasn't sick because she was ill but because she was 'making' herself sick. I knew what THAT meant so I jumped in the car without further ado and arrived at the school in record time. I was met by the matron in charge who really shocked me when she told me my daughter had been bulimic for some time but they had been unable to tell me until she herself felt ready to tell me. That particular night had been the night she had felt brave enough to do it - hence the telephone call. After much discussion it was decided I should take my daughter home for a few days.

The next day my daughter spent a lot of time in my arms, sobbing her heart out. She said that she now knew how much I loved her and that everything would be okay. She said she knew that I loved her because I had dropped everything in the middle of the night and gone to fetch her, even though she knew I was hurt because she hadn't told me about her bulimia. Something magical was happening between us and we were finding the most amazing and deep love for each other. Of course, I knew what had happened at both levels but the synchronization of it all quite overwhelmed me. I fell on my knees before the greater power and not only gave thanks for the miracle that was happening but also for the huge understanding I was receiving of how the two lives were connected and how this one was healing the last one. I was unable to tell my daughter because she did not desire that level of understanding but from that day to this, we have the most wonderful relationship and we love each other so very dearly.

Such absolute proof of the connection between the two lives served to deepen my ability to unearth more detail of that all important past life! I could not doubt that I was picking up the details accurately because I was watching two of my children heal in front of my eyes in their different ways. I started to think more broadly in terms of what was happening and to ask God who else was connected to all this and how they could be helped. One of the most important people of course was my husband and I really didn't know how to begin. But I knew deep down that I didn't have to worry because this whole thing was so much bigger than me and all that was supposed to happen would happen, in its own good time. I knew I had forgiven my husband the minute I knew of his involvement but I also knew he was carrying a huge load of problems relating to it and they could only be healed in the same way that my children were being healed. I told a couple of friends what I suspected was happening and I was quite amazed when I was not pooh-poohed! In fact, I received encouragement such as,

"It will all sort itself out in time!"

and,

"It doesn't surprise me at all."

So I courageously continued with all that life was throwing at me, ever more deeply becoming aware of the TWO WORLDS and starting to pick up helpful past lives for other people as well as my own family.

7

Spiritual tuition in the extraordinary

PEOPLE TALK OF SOUL MATES and twin souls quite freely these days and in doing so they are obviously feeling a very special close connection with another being. I have never found it too important to know exactly how I am connected with people at soul level, I simply know that there are different connections and they are closer at some moments than others. However, one soul mate connection that I was happy to acknowledge was with my godmother's son, Fred. I had known him most of my life because our mothers were close friends, despite the fact that his mother lived in Australia and mine lived in Great Britain. We had got to know each other really well when I was nineteen. I had gone out to stay with his family while they were living temporarily in Pakistan. We spent two months together, partly touring the local area around Islamabad, partly visiting India and Afghanistan, and partly experiencing the diplomatic life of the Australian embassy to which his father was attached. Our soul connection was interesting because my soul group had been shown to me as if it were beads fixed intermittently on a necklace, that was slowly turning, and I was shown that Fred's soul group was on a similar but separate necklace, travelling in the opposite direction, and the two necklaces were connecting like cogs on a wheel! I therefore called him my 'anti-cycle!' Looking through a cross section of our souls' lives I could see the two necklaces travelling round and creating a rub-off effect against each other over and over again, and it was always a beneficial learning experience for both parties. I believe this rub-off has also been happening through a number of earthly generations, and our families are deeply connected both spiritually and physically.

In 2001, Fred was brought back into my life in quite an extraordinary way. He was an elder at the Findhorn community and he had lived in a tiny old caravan there, since he was twenty. I felt an incredible urge to go and visit him and this was not an easy urge to comply with, given the distance I had to travel to get to him and my own family commitments. However, I found it would be possible for me to go in the autumn of that year and my mum was willing to keep an eye on the three children while I was away, which gave me great peace of mind.

Findhorn is situated in a very northerly part of Scotland and in an area that I had never visited before. I didn't know what to expect because I had heard so many weird and wonderful stories about the community, but I decided to go with a very open mind and to let the spiritual purpose of my visit unfold in its own way.

I found Fred's caravan quite easily and as I approached it, he was just coming out of it, so finding each other turned out to be fairly simple. We re-entered his caravan and had only been talking for an hour or so when I noticed that he was looking rather strange and he informed me that he might be going to have an epileptic fit. (Fred had been mugged in London many years previously and it had left him with severe epilepsy.) Taking a closer look at him, I could see there was sweat pouring down his face and he then started talking in half sentences. I anxiously asked him if he would like some healing. He nodded and allowed me to put my hand about four inches above the top of his head. I could feel an enormous rush of hot air coming out of his head moving fast towards the ceiling. I encouraged the heat out and nervously watched while Fred gradually returned to normal. After a while he remarked,

"I've never stopped a fit coming on before!"

We were both highly delighted and I felt incredibly relieved because I would have been way out of my depth if he had had a full blown attack. He then drank quite a few glasses of water and soon he was able to converse properly again.

I decided I would like to treat him to an evening meal at the local pub because he had very little food in his caravan and he didn't have any money to buy any more! We took the car because he felt unable to walk the small distance (about a mile) to the village where the pub was. If I had known him better I would have known this was a sign that all was not quite well with him, but I was blissfully ignorant, and we drove off happily, thinking the fit was well sorted out.

Once in the pub we sat at a wooden table opposite each other. Little did I know I was about to witness the most bizarre scene I could ever have imagined. Firstly, we started chatting about various family matters quite normally. But as we talked I noticed that his eyes were behaving a little oddly. They were rolling about and his eyeballs were twitching. I noticed that sweat was pouring down his face again. I wanted to say to him,

"Take off your hat!" hoping it would let out the same rush of hot air as before but it was a public place and I was a bit unsure of myself. Instead I said to him,

"Are you trying to fight it off?"

He nodded. We sat in silence for a little while and then he suddenly looked at me and said politely,

"Do I know you?"

Well I was flabbergasted! What sort of a statement was that? I didn't know what to answer but Fred was not looking for an answer, he was looking around the pub in an inquisitive type of way. I tentatively enquired,

"Fred, are you alright?"

He brought his gaze back to me and eventually said,

"Excuse me!"

He got up from the table and started to walk around the room, moving various beer mats and different people's glasses of beer in an abstracted and uncomfortable way. After a little while he came and sat down opposite me again. I looked at him and he smiled and proceeded to talk to me as if I were a complete stranger. I was getting extremely worried and wondered if I was watching him being taken over by another spirit. It certainly didn't appear to be Fred sitting in front of me any more! Presently, Fred got up again and I watched some more wanderings around the room, thinking that perhaps I should have a word with the publican to find out if this was normal 'Fred' behaviour. However before I could do anything, he suddenly went out of the pub door and I felt I must rush after him because I didn't want to lose him while he was in such a peculiar state. I followed him around outside for some time, he occasionally smiled at me but other than that we spoke no words. I simply didn't know what to say to him. Luckily for me, he eventually made his way back into the pub and I quickly said to the girl behind the bar that something strange was happening to my friend and I pointed him out to her as he skirted round some tables. She watched him for a little while and then, after consultation with her colleagues, it was decided to call an ambulance. I started to feel a little less panicky because I had some positive support.

The ambulance arrived fairly quickly. The medics did a quick assessment of Fred and then guided him toward the back of the ambulance. He got in so I quickly got into my car and drove behind the ambulance as it took Fred off to the local hospital. Once in the hospital I witnessed the worst attack of epilepsy that I ever want to see. The nurses were wonderful and knew exactly how to cope with him and eventually I left him in their capable hands and went off to find somewhere to stay the night.

An extraordinary couple of days followed because I found myself stranded at Findhorn knowing absolutely no-one, with Fred in hospital and all the worry of what had happened playing on my mind. But the universe knew exactly what it had planned for me and in the next forty eight hours I was led to meet various prominent members of the community. They were extremely friendly and kind to me and were able to help me understand what Fred's life was like and what he did for the community when he was well. Through the people I met I was able to conjure up a picture of Fred's daily life and I also began to understand how it must feel to live within the centre of such an unusual community. I felt that I met more of his fascinating friends and gained a far greater insight into the essence of Findhorn, than I would have done had I visited the place under more normal circumstances.

Later the next day, I decided to go and see how Fred was getting on in hospital. After the events of the previous evening I was rather apprehensive and I approached his bed cautiously. Who was he going to be? Would he recognise me? He smiled as I walked towards him and said,

"Hello!"

I breathed a huge sigh of relief because he was recognising me. Heavy doses of drugs over night had brought him out of the fit and rebalanced him. I started to tell him what had happened in the pub and he was absolutely amazed and said he didn't remember any of it. He listened with great interest to all I had to say and then declared that no-one had ever witnessed him being in that state before because he normally shut himself up in his caravan when he felt a fit coming on. He told me that he usually quite enjoyed his pre-fit states but he was unaware that he was probably being taken over by another spirit each time it happened. It was all a huge revelation to us both. He became aware of what was happening to him at a much deeper level and I felt I had witnessed the most incredible exchange of occupancy of his body, in front of my very eyes.

I stayed one more night in Findhorn, mostly because I wanted to try and improve Fred's living quarters while I had the chance, and also to try and strengthen the support systems around him. I made sure the people that mattered knew what I had seen and would try and help him in the future but they all made it clear to me that he was extremely difficult to help! However, I made some very valuable contacts for myself and came away feeling I had a good idea what the Findhorn foundation was all about. I did not feel I should like to be involved in it in any way but I certainly felt the people there were very lucky to have the support of each other in their every day spiritual lives and it highlighted the huge lack of it in mine. As I drove back down south, I wondered just why it had been necessary for me to experience all this and yet at the same time I marvelled at the way I had been led around the community, meeting exactly the right people at exactly the right time, enabling me to learn what I needed to learn, both for Fred's sake and for my own.

The next part of this story is bizarre in the extreme and I'm not sure how accurately I picked it up because I had never before had such an awkward story channelled through me. But it goes something like this:

Two days after I returned from Findhorn I was led into a very quiet spot and encouraged to be very still. This was not the first time this had happened to me so the feelings were not unfamiliar. However, I had no idea at all what was about to be revealed to me. I felt myself sink into another dimension completely and I became aware that Fred's brother was with me. Fred's brother, who I shall refer to as Mark, had died in a car accident when he was in his early twenties. The accident happened because he had drunk too much alcohol. I had never known him and I was more than surprised to find myself being addressed by him. He started to tell me he was very angry that his life had been terminated so young and he felt he had been wrongly robbed. He missed his earthly family enormously and he wanted to be with them. He spent a good deal of time around his mother but he was frustrated because he couldn't speak to her and get answers, although he knew she usually sensed when he was there. Not long after the accident had happened, he told me he had cottoned on to the idea that he could get back to this earth by dropping into vacant bodies when he saw they were available. Obviously, the only bodies that he really wanted to drop into were the ones connected to his own family, because they would bring him into contact with his loved ones again and thus help him out of his misery.

First of all he had tried to invade his older brother's body but his older brother was a very 'grounded' type of person and he found that he never got the right opportunity. So he began to try and invade Fred, and although Fred should have been a prime target because of his interest in the occult and other worlds, he was still unable to find a space to enter. So he told me he had the shocking idea of arranging for Fred to be mugged. Such was his desire to get back into the earthly world that he failed to see how damaging this would be to Fred. He was only aware of his desire to see his family again and he felt it was his right, because his life had been cut off so prematurely. So, Fred was duly mugged and Mark tried to enter. Unfortunately for Mark, the mugging was not severe enough because although Fred was left with dreadful headaches, there was still not enough access for Mark to gain an entry. Undaunted, Mark arranged for another mugging and this time he was successful. Fred's nerves were damaged at the back of his neck and he started to have epileptic fits. Fred's brother was able to see the fits coming and he realised that he could now effectively carry out a swap and occupy the space that Fred was moving out of. At the appropriate moment he would jump into Fred's body and have the earthly connection that he had been looking for.

I was very, very shocked! I could hardly believe what was being conveyed to me! After a small break in Mark's communication I tentatively asked,

"What do you want with me and why are you telling me all this?"

Mark told me that he was changing. His mother had recently had a stroke and it had left her suspecting that she may not have much longer to live. Mark was upset by his mother's distress because he could feel she was yearning to see Fred. The fits meant that his mother couldn't see Fred very often because he was unable to travel to Australia on his own and obviously, because of the stroke, she was now unable to travel to see him or even talk to him properly over the 'phone. Mark had now realised that he wanted to find a way to put things right. It was he who had planted in me the desire to visit Fred at Findhorn and arranged for me to witness the events that I had! He said he normally made sure that Fred was safe in his caravan before a fit so he could enjoy the pre-fit state, but he had decided to reveal it all to me in the pub because he knew it would bring it all out into the open. He had chosen me as the witness because he recognised that I was a spiritually evolved being who had learnt the right lessons in life to be able to help him. I was amazed and asked what he thought I could do. Firstly, he asked me if I thought he could ever be forgiven for what he had done. Well, this was easy and I replied,

"Of course you can! You are no more or less guilty than the rest of us when we are acting under an illusion. The most important thing is that you have seen the folly of your ways and want to redress it."

Mark then told me he was going to act like a guardian angel to Fred in the future and not allow any other spirits to enter the void that was left open, ahead of an epileptic fit, until Fred was well enough to stop them entering for himself. He said the pre-fit states in the future would allow spiritual inspiration for Fred's writing to come in. He also admitted that some of Fred's desire for alcohol had come from him and he would try and discourage him now and give him a desire to take the nutrients that his friends at Findhorn wished him to take. All in all, he wanted to get Fred well enough so that he would be able to travel to Australia and delight his mother's last days. His ultimate desire was to respond to his mother's yearning to see Fred and I knew he was truly, very sorry for what he had done. When he had put as much right as possible, he promised me he would move on and address his own soul's future, never bothering anyone on earth again.

It took me a long time to absorb what had been revealed to me that day and luckily I was able to talk it over with my mother. She declared that it was quite 'mind blowing' but at the same time it made so much sense and it explained why Fred had been mugged twice. For my part it was the first time that something so detailed and dramatic had ever been conveyed to me and it certainly opened the doors for further such communications in the future.

To complete Fred's story, you would probably like to know that he improved enough to visit Australia twice before he died. The first time he went with his aunt and uncle and successfully celebrated his parent's fiftieth wedding anniversary with them. The second time I took him over myself, some four years later, because I had a definite feeling his mother needed to see him again. We travelled via Bangkok and had a very interesting few days there. We were incredibly in tune in everything that we did which made for a very harmonious experience. One evening, while we were sitting in a restaurant, he announced that we would probably see much more of each other in the future. I felt he had got this very wrong but I didn't say it to him. We travelled on to Australia, and while I only stayed with his parents for a couple of days, he had the most marvellous month with them and had no fits while he was there. I accompanied him back to England at the end of his month and believe it or not he had a fit on the aeroplane as we took off! I was praising the universe for the timing of it because I was able to cope with it, with the aid of the air hostesses, far easier than his parents would have been able to. We were being very well looked after indeed!

I was unbelievably glad that I had made the effort to take Fred across to the other side of the world to his mother, because six months later an extremely violent epileptic fit ended his life unexpectedly. However, upon reflection, I felt that all that should have been accomplished in his life, had been accomplished!

But I didn't lose him! He had been right about seeing much more of each other in the future! I was very instrumental in the arrangements for his funeral in Findhorn and he appeared to me several times there. He has also remained very present in my life ever since, popping in and out at strategic moments. One day in particular, when I was walking the dogs in the woods, I was aware that he was walking beside me. I 'heard' him say, amongst other things,

"Why don't you bring the Findhorn message down south?" Well, that was certainly food for thought, as you will see!

8

The Universe brings
about BIG changes

By 2002, my relationship with my husband was really struggling. I felt suffocated by our life together and I had a strong conviction that I would have to do something about it but I just couldn't see what. At the same time my mother's health was deteriorating rapidly and I knew that she hadn't got much longer to live. Whilst sitting in her kitchen with her one day, I had a vision of ropes coming down from above (above being symbolic of heaven) and I had been told that they would be slowly pulling her up. I didn't share this knowledge with anyone else; I just continued to fulfil my own vows to look after her to the best of my ability and put her at the top of my list of priorities. As she became more dependent on me she became increasingly more time consuming, but that gave us the opportunity for many in depth chats. One such chat led me to realise that my mum had totally accepted me for who I was at last and our relationship was now completely healed. When we had come to the farm she had had to accept me unconditionally otherwise we would all have been miserable. She had done this and I, for my part, had put right the wrongs of my youth. I felt as if our souls had come to a place of ultimate acceptance, almost where they were becoming one, and that all we had set out to accomplish in this life, had been completed!

At this time I was turning increasingly inwards for solace and help, because everything tangible in my life seemed to be in such a mess. I started to uncover more of the past life as a witch and to be aware of other people around me who had also been involved. For instance, I became aware of far more detail around the bonfire scene. I knew my husband had been accompanied by two other soldiers when I had been burnt and that one of them was my current elder sister. My relationship with my sister at this time was not particularly good and I had always been surprised at how good her relationship was with my husband. I was given to understand that they would be feeling the past life connection at a deep level and it would be drawing them closer than they would normally have been.

I also became aware that the man I was living with, during the past life, had died when our son was quite young. He had been a hunting man, spending long hours in the woods with his fellow huntsmen, pursuing his interests. We had been devoted to each other but I had made the big mistake of not spending enough time with him. I had been too immersed in what I was doing as a healer, and that was one of the reasons he had departed from that life early. It felt as if he got fed up of waiting for me to come home in the evenings and decided he might as well depart from the life because I wasn't going to change. He was killed in some sort of hunting accident. I knew that this man was one of the few men I have ever really loved over my lives and that we had had many lives together. Part of me says that he, (or possibly she), will reappear in this life but I haven't knowingly come across him yet! If I do come across him, I know that I must give him more of my TIME!

With regard to my daughter, things were changing dramatically. I was finding she was inviting me to watch her hockey matches and to attend her school plays. She wanted to come shopping with me and volunteered to carry my bags. She was changing so much in her attitude towards me that I was almost overwhelmed at the healing that she had received. I couldn't help feeling that if SHE had had such a great healing, it would be possible to heal other relevant relationships too.

I was constantly uncovering a new depth of understanding within my younger son's life too. He was an exceptionally talented sportsman but he could never perform to his potential at school. I began to realise that he was afraid to stand out amongst his peers and his inner self was telling him that any success would be fatal. He always tried to blend in quietly amongst everyone, feeling he would be safer. As we uncovered the past life and realised how afraid he had been to be 'seen' after my death, his problems became understandable. Gradually, as we talked enough about it all and received help from a specialist in dyslexia, he began to heal and I am pleased to say that his last year at school was almost happy. He was actually 'man of the match' a few times on the cricket field.

In August 2003, while my mother was still able to look after herself, although she was increasingly needing assistance, I suddenly cracked and asked my husband to leave. He was beside himself and begged me to rethink, promising to improve his ways. I felt absolutely terrible and, after considering the situation for a further twenty four hours, agreed to give him one more chance. Almost within days of this happening my mother took a real turn for the worse and she died on the second of November that year. Her death was a terrible blow for us all, because by this time we had been living together on the same property for about seven years and had become incredibly close. My husband was unbelievably kind during this time, and such a huge rock of comfort, that getting through the next few weeks would have been much harder without him. But the hole that my mother left seemed almost too much to cope with and her departure also changed the dynamics of the relationships between my sisters and myself and my husband and myself so much, that my mind was almost blown.

One important incident I recall, took place a couple of days after my mother had died. I was sitting in her kitchen when the most enormous feeling of fear rose up in me and I became completely hysterical. I was aware of something terribly black and frightening that I would have to face. My elder sister, who was sitting opposite me, was witness to the INDESCRIBABLE fear that showed itself in my body for a moment and then died down again, leaving us both rather shaken, knowing it had happened but not knowing what it meant. But we did both know that it came from a deeper source than just the death of my mother and that it had probably shown itself then because something in my subconscious recognised that my mother was no longer around to protect me.

From the day of my mother's death, the speed of my spiritual growth accelerated rapidly. It was obvious from the first that her departure had been perfectly timed and from her new position she was going to be able to help me far more than she had been able to, whilst still in her body. I had a great deal of communion with her and often felt a strong sensation of her loving presence.

It was literally only ten days after mum's departure that she caused me to meet someone who was to change my life completely. I was walking the dogs through the woods, feeling utterly miserable, when I saw a man ahead of me, hanging a hammock between two trees. As I drew closer to him I heard my mother's voice saying to me,

"Now, be very, very nice to him."

I remembered how she had smiled bravely at all the nurses in the hospital, despite her pain, right up to her death and I thought to myself,

"Well if she can do that, I can be nice to people too, even though I don't feel like it!"

So I stopped and smiled at the man and asked him what he was doing. We had a chat for a little while and he told me he was writing a book on survival. When I showed interest in it he promised to let me have a copy. I went on my way not thinking much more about the incident, and certainly not aware of the tremendous rapport he had felt with me.

Over the next few weeks I seemed to come across this man in all sorts of places in the woods, sometimes I was with my sister and sometimes not. My sister took an instant dislike to him and told me not to have anything to do with him but I replied that I was quite flattered by his attentions and thought he was rather nice. She insisted he was bad news, so I started to be careful where I met him and to hide our meetings from her. I do remember my mum communicating to me very clearly,

"Be careful, he's not the one for you!"

I was extremely puzzled by this, because I knew she had wanted me to meet him .So I reservedly continued to meet him and unfortunately, after a few months, fell in love with him. I had never been in love before and the situation, coming on top of mum's death, was almost unmanageable! But luckily we were all so emotionally churned up after mum's death that I could hide the turmoil going on inside me fairly easily.

My new man, who I shall call Graham, was not a very balanced individual and had I not been in such deep mourning I might have realised it sooner. However all I was really aware of was that I had definitely known him in a previous life and we had been greatly in love. The closest he got to recognising this connection was to ask me if we had ever met before because he felt he knew me!

Over the next few months I met Graham for walks fairly regularly but I started to be very puzzled that he never seemed to want more than this. He never kissed me but we had wonderful hugs and he made me feel amazing. He told me all sorts of stories about his life in the Parachute Regiment and I listened to him happily because it was something new and different, and was taking me away from the painful situation at home. Meeting him was very difficult to arrange, not so much because the situation was secret, but because Graham was unable to make what most people would call 'normal' arrangements. He never seemed to be able to commit to a definite time or place and would leave me wondering when I was next going to see him for long periods of time. He said it was because of his job as a private detective but for someone as deeply in love as I was, and as he appeared to be, it left me in much more distress than was good for me. So I knew fairly quickly that I could not rely on him for any support but my life was so disturbed generally, that I allowed the situation to continue. Also I never knew what he was going to be like when I did meet him because sometimes he was superb company and sometimes he was in a dreadful mood and I was not always able to coax him out of it. As our association continued, I felt certain that Graham had not had many lives recently and that he had been in a dark place for a long time in the spirit world. I felt that this was why he didn't cope with this life very well and why he lived a lot of his life, not accepting the twenty first century, preferring to harp back to the 'olden day' ways in which he felt more comfortable. But, however difficult it all was, deep within me I knew I was supposed to be meeting him, and I continued to do so through thick and thin.

Most of 2004 passed in a blur for me. Not only did I have the situation with Graham to contend with but my marriage was a continual source of anxiety and tension. Now that I had fallen in love and experienced the feelings involved with that emotion, I knew for certain I had never loved my husband in the same way. However, he insisted that he loved me in that way and it was such a puzzle to me. How could it be so one way? At the same time I was coping with the, 'oh so painful' loss of my mother and the new dynamics that it threw up. As if all that wasn't enough, my sisters worked out that there would not be enough money left by my mother for me to stay at the farm, so it appeared that I was going to lose my home too. My children were all completing their various educations and were looking to leave home in the near future. Everything, just everything, was up in the air! The positive side to it all, because there always is a positive side, was that I had to learn to live for the moment rather than to worry about what the future would hold. It was the only way I could begin to exist and at one stage I was only able to survive by living one minute at a time!

My trip to Australia had been arranged for November of that year, and not only did I plan to take Fred with me, as pre-arranged, but I decided to invite Graham to come too. I thought we could spend some quality time together and that I could try and find out who he really was, without hurting or bothering anyone else. As the time approached to leave, I increasingly felt I would not be able to do this trip whilst still in my marriage and so I told my husband that I didn't want to sleep with him any more and I made a bedroom for myself elsewhere in the house. I hurt him unbearably by doing this but the move started to bring my situation out into the open as never before! He started to question me in all sorts of ways and as I was unable to lie, the truth began to emerge. Unfortunately, because I was being so open, many other people began to get involved in our unhappy situation. My older sister could not come to terms with my association with Graham at all and it seemed to me that she sided with my husband and eventually needed to turn her back on the family for quite a few months during this period. She did this for her own sake because affairs had gone beyond what she could cope with. There was also an acquaintance of ours called Derek who decided to get involved, and instead of helping us, he made the situation a lot worse by interfering beyond what was reasonable and in a seemingly dishonest way. He ended up managing to set my husband and I against each other in unnecessary ways so that it was more difficult for us to navigate our way out of our mess. I couldn't think why this was happening at the time but later realised that Derek had his own problems and his own issues were causing him to act in this unhelpful way. Various other people were in and out of the situation, including a therapist that I went to see because everything was overwhelming me.

Despite all the trauma around us, I decided to go ahead with my trip to Australia, mainly because I did not want to let Fred down. I wasn't certain if Graham would meet me in Darwin, because I hadn't seen him for quite a long time but I decided I would benefit enormously from the experience of travelling on my own in a foreign country and I bravely set off, leaving the future of everything in the safe hands of the universe. I had left a terrible situation behind me at home, and I didn't know for the life of me how to sort it out.

In the event, my entire trip proved to be unbelievably stressful. It was extremely scary taking an epileptic from one side of the world to the other and I was nervous the entire journey, especially on our stop over in the chaotic city of Bangkok. However, I managed to deposit Fred safely with his parents, stayed with the family for a couple of days, and then made my way to Darwin. As soon as I got to the hotel in Darwin I found Graham had already booked into my room and was lying on the bed in a terrible state. I did not know what was causing his desperately irrational state of mind and I was faced with a man I hardly recognised and, I realised very quickly, one I hardly wanted to know. He produced some very peculiar items from his rucksack; two of these were enormous knives which he said he was going to use when we went into the bush. Initially I was scared stiff at the thought of sharing a room with those huge knives but something inside me told me that I probably wasn't in danger myself but that if he got into one of his moods/tempers, someone else might be. I looked at the rest of his kit which was unusual in the extreme, more as if he was going on a military mission than on a holiday. I wondered what on earth I had got myself into and my whole being was immersed immediately in a prayer for the 'highest good' to prevail. Of course I couldn't tell anyone else what was going on and it was a huge strengthening process for me, having to cope with it all, completely on my own.

Over the next few days I discovered Graham didn't want to leave the hotel room much and if I wanted to see anything of Darwin I would be doing it alone. This situation was entirely new for me because everything

I had done to date had been in a family environment and very protected. However I put my best foot forward and did as much sight seeing as I possibly could. Eating was a real problem because Graham felt unable to enter most of the restaurants because he thought he could see evil people in them and that we would be in some sort of danger if we went in. Therefore, I learnt to find very quiet places where people didn't pose a threat to him. I always had to let him choose where we ate. If I chose, things undoubtedly went wrong and the tension it created in him made him shout at the waiters or anyone else who came near. It was incredibly embarrassing and I started to avoid these situations whenever I saw them coming.

After five days in Darwin we were due to travel south to Alice Springs. I woke up in the morning and suddenly decided that I couldn't put up with the terrible tension that Graham created any longer and I wanted to do the rest of the holiday alone, even though I was in a foreign country and very scared of being on my own. I got up very quickly, packed my bags and left the hotel room, saying to Graham as I departed that he was to travel on his own now and I was going to do my own thing. I vaguely registered his surprise as I rushed out of the door and my heart was beating furiously in case he tried to stop me. However I think that the element of surprise was such that he was totally unprepared for my departure in this way and I left the hotel room safely. Once alone, I felt completely protected by the spirit world and I knew that all that was happening was for the highest good, even though I was really nervous. I had a real bubble of joy in my heart as I walked down the street and bought a few post cards and some breakfast. I wandered around the shops and then made my way to the bus station ready to take the bus to Alice Springs.

I sat down on a seat at the front of the bus and soon realised that Graham was sitting in another seat a little way behind me. I was half relieved and half bothered. I decided to ignore him and the first leg of the journey passed uneventfully enough. But at the first stop over he alighted from the bus after me and started to follow me down the road to the hotel. I asked him why he was following me and he replied that he had come to Australia to be with me and he wasn't going to leave me now. I told him his behaviour was unbearable and that I had decided I would be better off without him. He simply said he would do his utmost to improve. I reluctantly gave in and we booked in together at the hotel. In the event, it turned out that my abandonment of him at the previous hotel had shaken him greatly and caused a massive turning point in his subsequent thinking and behaviour. He did his very best to behave himself and although it was a slow process, I could see the tremendous effort he was making and I encouraged him as much as I could. I discovered he really struggled in a crowd of any sort and if I could keep him away from other people as much as possible, he was more able to relax and enjoy himself. I started to plan the trip in a way that he could cope with and as I improved in reading his needs, he improved in his temperament and ability to be a companion. About half way through the holiday we hired a car and he enjoyed doing the driving and obviously felt good about himself behind the wheel. We did a few day trips like walking in the mountains and taking a boat out. As he managed to relax more, the trips became enjoyable, though still a strain, in case he suddenly couldn't cope with something or a person irritated him and then we would have to abandon what we were doing. As I could never quite predict when he was going to blow up, I never managed to totally relax myself.

I had come to Australia with this man to gain experience of him and by golly was I doing that! But I was also feeling the continual presence of the spirit world in a very strong way, sometimes so strongly that I felt I was floating in the air. I was being totally guided and taken care of in everything that happened. I knew I was giving Graham an opportunity that he had never experienced before and that a huge healing was taking place because of my continual unconditional love. By the time we got to the last three days his behaviour was almost as normal as the average man in the street and we had the greatest fun together. He still left me to do a lot of things on my own and by this time I had learnt to give him all the space that he needed. During this period he started to say repeatedly that he didn't want to go home and I could understand why. He was probably the happiest he had ever been in his life at this point and he didn't want it to end. However we were due to meet Fred at the airport, which we duly did, and our return journey began. I wouldn't say it was an easy journey. Graham reverted to type in the presence of Fred and became much more difficult again. He hated our stop over in the States and threw abuse at a lot of the Americans that we encountered because he couldn't cope with the busy city of Los Angeles. Fred, of course, had his epileptic fit on the aeroplane which had to be dealt with, so I basically arrived back at Heathrow pretty exhausted and not having had a minute to think how I was going to face the future at home.

The next few months were probably the most emotionally painful ones my husband and I could ever experience. When I got home I related to the family a little of what had happened in Australia and did not hide the fact that Graham had been with me. I did however make it clear to everyone that he and I would never have a permanent relationship but I don't think I was believed. I was still being guided on a minute to minute basis by the spirit world and therefore I did not look beyond the moment in which I was living. I couldn't! So much was happening and there was so much pain being experienced. I told my husband I no longer wanted to sleep with him because our relationship had always been one sided and that it was time for me to find out the truth of WHO I REALLY WAS and WHAT I SHOULD BE DOING! He was devastated and said he could not live with me if I would not be a proper wife to him in every sense of the word. Unbelievably I stuck to my guns and I knew now why my mother had wanted me to meet Graham. It wasn't that I was to have a permanent relationship with him; he simply wasn't capable of it, but my falling in love with him had given me the strength that I had never had before, to stand up to my husband and face the truth of our 'flawed' relationship. I acknowledged openly that our marriage was a 'living lie' in some way and I knew that I had to redress it if I was ever going to find myself, in the truest sense of the word!

My husband was as miserable as any one could possibly be. He could hardly believe all this was happening and he continued to state that I had married him for better or worse and that I should sleep in his bed. I privately thought that if he really loved me he would be prepared to give me the space that I needed but he could not see it that way at all. Therefore we looked for another house for him to live in and found one that was only half an hour's drive away from the farm. In April 2005 he moved into it. I say he moved into it but it is truer to say that I moved him out of the farm. He was not capable of packing up his stuff or the furniture that he needed, it all had to be done by me! He was feeling so hurt and so wronged, that he could hardly put one foot in front of the other. We also had the problem of Derek, the interfering acquaintance and until I persuaded my husband to stop listening to him and to do things in a way that WE wanted, we had many added difficulties.

To explain as much as one is able to explain these things, I will tell you that the enormity of being left on my own, on a one hundred and ten acre farm, with no male support was almost totally overwhelming. Within an hour of my husband's departure I started to hyperventilate and was unable to do more than lie on a chair in the garden for the next few days while I learnt to control it. It was quite some time before I could breathe completely normally again and do anything much more than look after the animals and myself. I felt the HUGE comfort of the universe around me and I knew with absolute certainty that however bad I was feeling, I was doing the right thing. I was extremely worried about my husband and wanted to 'phone him every moment but managed not to do it too often! He was struggling enormously by himself, and hardly took any interest in his surroundings and new home. It was a terrible time for us both. However, as we still owned a lot of sheep, he had to come back over to the farm on a regular basis and we were forced to start sorting out a new way of managing our lives very quickly.

9

Drawn to Findhorn and experiencing a fast forwarding process

ONE OF THE MOST NOTABLE things that happened during the summer of 2005 was the unexpected death of my dear friend Fred. He had been back at Findhorn since our return from Australia but had not been particularly well, having suffered some very severe epileptic fits. However, by April he had started to recover, and was trying to pick up the reins of his life again. He was looking forward to celebrating his fiftieth birthday in July.

One day in June, I was contacted by a lady from Findhorn, who informed me that Fred had died very suddenly, after a particularly severe epileptic fit. I had the unenviable task of informing his parents who were living in Australia. Fortunately the lady was able to contact Fred's daughter, Penelope, who was working on the island of Iona for the summer. I decided to send Penelope a text to ask if there was anything I could do to help her and she replied,

"Yes, please! Where do I start? I don't know what to do?"

There was a huge amount of anguish conveyed in those few statements and I knew I had to support her. My own daughter, who was almost the same age as Penelope, was jumping up and down beside me, insisting;

"Mum, she's all on her own, she has no other family, you must go and help her. I'll look after the farm!"

I knew Fred's parents would be unable to fly over from Australia as his mother had been left severely handicapped from the stroke. I contacted his only other relatives in the U.K. and they were unable to go to her so I got in my car, there and then, and started the long drive north to Findhorn.

The uncanny thing about this second visit to Findhorn was the extreme circumstances which once again surrounded it. I was to spend another few days being led from one person to another experiencing more of the core of the Findhorn community. I was invited to stay in a caravan with a lady who lived opposite Fred, which was situated in the heart of the foundation. She had several bedrooms in her caravan which she let out, so we arranged for Penelope and her boyfriend to stay there too.

I arrived at Findhorn before Penelope and while I waited for her, I got to know my hostess over a cup of coffee. She had known Fred for a very long time and had been very fond of him. She also knew Penelope much better than I did and was able to give me all sorts of information about her and also about how to start arranging the funeral. She knew all the right people to visit and telephoned them all for me, to arrange a time for Penelope and I to meet them. So when Penelope finally arrived, we were able to go calmly around the foundation, arranging the funeral day in exactly the way she wanted.

The whole experience was quite surreal. The Findhorn community was clearly shocked by Fred's death and wanted to help in every way they could. We even had a few minutes with Eileen Caddy, the co-founder of the community, and although she was too old to do anything to help, her support and love were strongly felt by us both. We met many of Fred's closest friends and I learnt significantly more about him and how he had interacted with his fellow community members. Penelope leaned on me heavily for a type of motherly, emotional support but as we went around the place, meeting various people, she knew in her own mind, exactly what she wanted to do for the funeral. She felt her father strongly guiding her at times and I also was certainly aware of his presence. I suppose one of the most important things I picked up as we made our way round, was the calm atmosphere of the place. I experienced deeply how community members interacted with each other, how they supported and loved everyone equally, accepting each other without question for who they were. I had never felt anything quite like it, anywhere else!

During one of our conversations I learnt that there

was a sanctuary for anyone needing a quiet place to pray. I wanted very much to have a look at it but we were so busy, it did not seem as if I would have the opportunity. However, I decided that as I wanted to see it so much, I would go late at night, when Penelope, her boyfriend and I had finished making our arrangements for the day. I set off with a set of directions from my hostess, knowing I was looking for a big roundish building but it proved to be quite difficult to find because I didn't know the area and it was midnight! Eventually I came across it, tucked quietly away amongst several other buildings.

As I approached the sanctuary, for some reason I felt quite excited. I gingerly opened the door and looked inside, feeling glad that no-one else was in there. I stood just inside the door for a little while, noticing first that the atmosphere was not quite as peaceful as I had expected. I could feel the busy energy that its many visitors must have left there; it was crossing and recrossing the building. I gazed around, taking in the unusual format of the place. Basically it had a lighted candle in the centre of the floor and a few cushions placed in a circle around the candle. Around the cushions were three circles of chairs getting bigger with each circle, the last one having the backs of the chairs set against the circular walls. I decided to sit in a chair in the second row and have a little time to myself.

As I sat there, quite oblivious of time, many thoughts came to me, but one of the most bizarre was that each circle of seats represented how close one was to the candle, in one's life. The candle for me at that moment represented Eileen Caddy, who was very much at the heart of Findhorn. I looked at where I was sitting in the middle row of chairs and I felt I was probably in the right place. I felt I was beyond the back row but not yet ready for the front row and certainly nowhere near the cushions!

I pondered over these strange thoughts and started to question myself.

"Would I like to be able to advance to the next set of chairs?" I paused for thought.

"Yes, I would!"

And I decided to ask God if I could work towards that in the future. After a while I thought,

"If I sit in one of the inner circle chairs I might get a feeling of how the future looks!"

I got up hesitantly, moved myself forward into the inner circle and finally sat in one of the chairs. I felt quite uncomfortable to start with but as the minutes ticked by, I settled down and started to relax. I knew for definite I would like to feel a proper part of that circle and before too long, I did!

So there I was, sitting in the inner circle, feeling that I had made a definite statement about my future. But then another idea struck me as I looked at the cushions in front of me. I thought naughtily,

"I wonder if I'll ever get that close to the candle!"

In that instant I knew I wanted to and I felt the urge to go and sit on a cushion! I sat for a long time thinking about this and mostly feeling totally unworthy and yet wanting to be worthy! Eventually I got up and sat on a cushion! I looked around feeling almost guilty. What was I doing?

I don't know how much time past in that position.

I only know that I was acutely aware of the candle flickering in front of me. I felt it epitomized Eileen and all her prayers over the years. I could feel her strength, her solitude and the enormous faith she had, that had created the community as it was at that time. My respect for her was total. Watching the candle glimmer I knew that I did not want to follow in her shoes but that I would like to be used in a similar way, elsewhere! I felt enormous admiration for her and all she had achieved but I knew my own path would be a little different.

I was drawn more and more towards that single flame as I sat in silence in that much used, but currently empty, sanctuary. I looked around and wondered if anyone could see in from the outside. It appeared that they could not. I then looked at the door and wondered if anyone else would come in. Obviously, anyone could come in, at any time. I sat there sweating slightly, for I had an impulse to move myself towards the candle. What should I do? Eventually, after a quick look round to make sure the door was still shut, I got up and manoeuvred myself onto my hands and knees with the flame under me. I quietly said,

"Thy will be done!"

I stayed there for a short while, very aware of the flickering candle beneath me, every bone and sinew oozing my simple prayer. Then I moved back to one of the cushions, breathing very fast. It had been an extremely special moment and one that I felt had HUGE meaning for me. I sat for a few minutes longer contemplating what had passed, then stood up and quietly let myself out of the sanctuary.

No-one was around as I made my way back to the

caravan I was staying in, for which I was heartily glad. I didn't feel like talking to any-one at that particular moment. I could only wonder with awe at what had happened. I also felt a little bit foolish!!

The next day dawned bright and I put the events of the previous night to the back of my mind. Penelope and I continued with the arrangements for the funeral, and I continued to meet all sorts of interesting people. I felt I made some excellent friends and renewed my acquaintance with some people whom I had met on my previous visit. We had managed to make contact with some of Fred's relatives by this time and Penelope's uncle let us know he would be arriving the next day from Australia. I felt strongly that when he arrived I would no longer be needed. My job was done!

As I drove south again from Findhorn I knew that Fred had been very present in everything we did. He was arranging his funeral as he wanted and he was guiding all his friends and family from his space in space! I also felt I had definitely been meant to go to Findhorn both for my own sake and for the sake of Penelope and the universe had used the opportunity well. I wondered what it would all mean for the future!

10

A terrible twist in the tale

IT IS AN IMPORTANT PART of this narrative to relate the tremendous twist in its tale that my relationship with Graham had, because of the interesting past life it brought up. Literally, only two days after my husband had left the farm, I tried to visit Graham at his home because he was being so unreasonable to me at a time when I really needed all the support I could get. I desperately wanted him to stop thinking only of himself and to try to understand how his outbursts were making my life so much more difficult. I knew it was happening because he was simply incapable of coping with everything I was going through so I wanted to try and enlist the help of his parents, if at all possible. Graham himself was out, when I arrived at the house but his parents were there and asked me in. They could see straight away that I was hyperventilating and in a very bad way. I tried to tell them what was happening to me and to explain that I understood that all Graham's experiences in the Parachute Regiment had made him the way he was and that I didn't blame him at all but could they possibly help him to be more reasonable at this very painful time. His parents looked at me in wide eyed amazement and his father said,

"He has never been in the parachute regiment!"

There was a prolonged stunned silence when even a pin dropping would have sounded like a bomb exploding! Eventually I stammered,

"What do you mean?"

His father said, "Has he told you that he served in the Paras?"

I managed to squeak out a tiny, "yes."

I was struggling to take in what this might mean.

"Oh dear," said his father. "He has told this type of lie before. I thought he had stopped doing it but now it appears that he hasn't."

The shock of what his father was saying stopped me hyperventilating completely for that moment! I looked from one of Graham's parents to the other in complete disbelief.

"Are you telling me that all the stories he has told me about his life in the Army are fabricated? That everything I know about him is false? Has he no connection with the forces at all?"

"I don't know what he's told you," said his father, "but he has definitely never been in the Army."

And over the next couple of hours his parents told me who Graham really was and what he had actually done with his life and my poor brain could hardly take it in. He had completely fabricated an entire lifestyle that had never existed and I had believed him! In actual fact, very little that I knew about him was true and one of the most stunning revelations was that before he had gone to Australia, he had never been in an aeroplane and had never been abroad! No wonder he had been in such a state when I found him in Darwin. He had just crossed the world by himself and managed to do it on his own, knowing he wasn't really capable of it! HE knew this but I DIDN'T!!

It took me many weeks to unravel what was revealed to me that day. Therefore, at the same time as coping with the immensely painful break up of my marriage I had to cope with this terrible deception. I had to accept that the man I thought I knew didn't exist and that the real one had quite a serious personality disorder. I knew my love for him was on a very different level to this earthly one and that it would transcend all his lies and deceptions in due course, but I had to come out of the shock that it had created in me. For instance, I wondered how much danger I had actually been in when I had traversed Australia with a man possessing two knives and such a dishonest, rocky personality. However, his father had assured me that whatever Graham threatened, he would actually never harm a fly. I now know this is true, but I certainly didn't at the time! I went through wave after wave of emotional shock as I relived all the stories he had told me and tried to come to terms with the truth. My whole being was one enormous prayer for help because there was nothing else I could do! And of course the help came..............

I forget exactly how it happened but I was taken into one of my 'altered' states and shown a past life where Graham and I had known each other. He had been a ruler of some sort in Egypt and had lived in an enormous palace. I had been the daughter of a humble woman living in a nearby town. I felt it was many centuries ago. I was not shown how he and I had met but I knew he visited me at my home in secret and that we were very much in love. My mother was very anxious about the situation but she felt she couldn't interfere in any way because of his status.

The country we lived in was at war and there came a time when Graham needed to turn his attentions seriously to addressing the nations problems and he did not have time to visit me. But I was a young maid in love and I did not understand how anything could be more important than seeing me! One day, feeling I could wait no longer for him to come to me, I left the house and ran through the side streets until I came to the palace gates. I could hear my mother calling after me,

"Don't go, don't go!"

But I ignored her and ran all the faster. When I got to the huge palace gates I took hold of them and shook them fiercely, screaming that I wanted to be let in to see Graham. I was totally out of control, creating a dreadful, noisy scene. Eventually one of the soldiers on the gate let me in and I was escorted up to the palace and immediately dumped in a dungeon. I wasn't at all worried. I felt sure that Graham would come and find me and I waited in hope and trust. One day, some soldiers came to fetch me and I was taken on a long journey which ended up in a very large cave. I climbed out of the cart that I had travelled in and looked around. There was a huge expanse of water in the cave and a biggish boat was moored close to the rocks, near the place I was standing. I saw Graham coming towards me and my heart filled with joy. As he approached, he explained that the country was now at war and that it was too dangerous for me to stay around. For my own safety he wanted me to get on the boat which would take me to a safe place where he would join me as soon as he could. I looked trustingly up at him and got on the boat as instructed. As the boat sailed out of the cave towards open waters, I suddenly became aware that the cabin I was in was filling with water and there was no way I could open the door. I started to shout hoping someone could hear me but nobody came and the water just went on coming in. The boat sank and of course I sank with it, drowning, as Graham had always intended. It was his way of putting as kind an end as he could to an embarrassing situation.

Deep in my 'altered' state I then became aware that our spirits were very close. I wanted to forgive him for what he had done and I asked him to forgive me for putting him in an awkward situation and for behaving so unreasonably! We hugged in this very deep place and I knew that it would be the start of healing Graham in this life.

At this stage I was seeing Graham occasionally but not telling him that I knew about his deception. It seemed his parents had not mentioned my visit to their house either. I knew I would have to discuss his deception at some point and that sooner would be better than later. I realised that it would probably mean I would never see him again but as I could never live a lie, I was obliged to take that risk. I continually asked

God for the best possible way for it to be achieved.

One day, when I was visiting Graham at his house, he started telling me some obvious lies and I found myself exclaiming,

"You mustn't do this any more!"

I told him very gently a little of what I knew and he went very quiet for a while and then suddenly burst out,

"I knew this would happen if I let myself get close to you!"

I knew exactly what he meant. For the first time in his life he had allowed his emotions a little rein and he had become fond of someone. Now his biggest fear had been realised. He felt I was about to betray his trust and he knew it was his own fault and he felt utterly miserable. I assured him that I still loved him and that it didn't matter about the lies. All that mattered was that he was now truthful with me. He couldn't take my assurances in at all. I believe all he could think was that I would now run a mile from him and he would have lost me for ever. He could not begin to see anything rationally as he fought an internal battle with his own guilt.

I spent the next few months getting accustomed to being on the farm on my own and all the work that it entailed. At the same time I was periodically seeing a very angry Graham. It was obvious that he didn't want to lose my friendship but he couldn't cope with me knowing what I knew. He simply didn't understand how I could forgive him and he was full of anger towards everything and everyone. I knew if I could ride the storm it would be a massive turning point for him, so I stuck to giving him my unconditional love throughout it all. He said and did some terrible things to me and at times my role was unbelievably hard.

After a very busy summer spent mostly working long, hard hours on the farm, I had the opportunity to go to Egypt with a group of spiritual people. I felt very drawn towards going as I had always wanted to see the pyramids and go on a boat trip down the Nile. Everyone thought it would be a good idea for me to get away so I booked it up. It proved to be an extremely challenging experience but the only thing I want to bring to your attention at this point is the fact that when we visited the Valley of the Kings, I could not get Graham out of my head. I felt as if he was there or had been there at some point. Shortly afterwards, I received a revelation that after he had died in the past life that I had already been made aware of, he had been buried in a tomb somewhere near, if not in, the valley. He had apparently lived the remainder of his life after my death feeling really miserable about what he had done to me and had, for the most part, been unable to come to terms with it. When he died, his soul had remained inside his tomb for a very long time, possibly centuries, deeply incarcerated in black energy because he felt he was unworthy of going to the light. After these revelations, all that I had suspected about him suddenly fell into place. I now understood why our meeting at the deep level when we had hugged each other, was such a huge turning point for him. I understood why he was mentally struggling so much in this life and why my unconditional love over the last few years was such an important part of his healing process. I began to see that our meeting in this life had been very 'intended' for he had come at exactly the right moment to help me out of my marriage and I had come to release him from his past life dungeon. I felt very, very happy as I thought through all that had happened to us both and marvelled at how I had been shown how the two lives interwove with each other.

My friendship with Graham has continued at a very light level since then and it has been marvellous to watch him improve and become a much happier person. He hasn't lost his temper with me for well over eighteen months now and is very pleasant company when we are together. It took him a long time to realise and accept that I actually love him for who he is and not for what he pretended to be. And as his confidence grows, he is becoming so much more balanced! For my part, my friendship with him has given me an in depth understanding of personality disorders in a very useful way and I have subsequently been able to help many other people.

But my revelations concerning Graham had not finished! About twelve months ago I was trying to help my older sister sort out her connection to me as a soldier in my past life as a witch, when it was revealed that the third soldier present at my death was Graham! I was extremely surprised, never having suspected he had been part of that life. The following scene was shown to me:

My husband (in this life) was in charge of the whole affair and had been the first to arrive at the scene of the bonfire on which I was to be burnt. He didn't know me personally but he had a natural hatred of witches, believing them to be evil, low, worthless creatures, as did many people in those days. He caught sight of me tied up nearby and decided that, as no-one else was around, he would have his way with me. He knew he didn't have much time because the other two soldiers were close behind him, so he tore the clothes off me and raped me extremely quickly. My sister (soldier) arrived at the scene with Graham (second soldier) close behind her and as they saw what was going on, Graham tried to brush past my sister to come to my rescue. He had some sort of horrible fight with my sister and she managed to prevent him from getting to me.

Suddenly, as the whole meaning of this dawned on me, I felt an incredible love for Graham and my heart glowed and glowed because I knew he had tried to save me from that terrible situation. Everything started to become clear at once. I realised why my sister had such a violent dislike of Graham when they first met. Of course she did! Her last contact with him had been a ghastly fight! I prayed earnestly for this hatred to now be resolved if at all possible! I then realised why my husband and I struggled so much with our sexual life; how could we not? Our last contact had been a rape! I pray that we will both be released from the bondage it has left us with in due course.

As I mulled over all these events and revelations I knew that though Graham had failed to save me in that life, he had agreed before we were born, to try save me again in this life and had been successful! Thus he had resolved some of his karma but the mystery of our two lives is still unfolding……………………..

11

A massive growth spurt and the 'gang' is introduced

I<small>F</small> I <small>WAS HOPING THAT</small> life was going to become any easier after my husband left I was sadly wrong, but I was certainly becoming happier as the summer of 2005 came to a close and autumn approached. Life on my own gave me time for reflection which I had never seriously had before and which was drawing me into a closer and closer union with God/source! My trip to Egypt certainly helped speed up my spiritual progress. It opened my eyes in umpteen new ways as I toured the ancient temples and pyramids and cruised down the Nile with my fellow companions. It was my first experience of spending time with other spiritual people in any serious way and I really struggled with the intensity of it. My path had always been very isolated until then, and I was totally unused to sharing my thinking with anyone else. But this trip was all about opening me up and hard kicks seemed to come from every direction!

One of the most interesting aspects was that all my travelling companions seemed to have a 'special' spiritual interest of some sort and were keen to share it. For instance there was a numerologist who said I was a 'nine' and proceeded to explain to me how she had worked it out and what it meant. There was an angel card reader who introduced me to the concept of angels and their uses, and I had some wonderful communication with angels while I was on the Nile which have helped me ever since. There were also people knowledgeable in herbal remedies and various incenses who advised me which would be beneficial and so on. I was very interested in all they had to say because I knew very little about their specialities. But I believe they all thought that I was a very young spiritual soul just starting out on my quest! They encouraged me to investigate the various avenues that were around for myself, to see what I would like to do. Deep inside I was resisting this, for I knew that the universe had always steered me clear of such things. This had puzzled me greatly at first but I later discovered that my path in this life lay in quite a different direction for I had done most or all of these 'trades' in past lives. Although I still didn't know my true life purpose for this life, I was growing closer to knowing, as each day passed. But of course my daily communication with these people was invaluable and I learnt and learnt and learnt! The intensity of being with them constantly, and visiting very powerful Egyptian sites, gave me an upset tummy for the duration of the trip and for a few weeks afterwards, but I was told this was normal and that I was 'processing'.

I settled back home after my Egyptian experience quite a changed person. I was still living very much in the moment, for this was the only way I had been able to survive for the last year and it was becoming second nature to me. My elder sister had by this time reconnected herself with the family and together we discussed the future of the farm and what my options were. It was clear that running a farm was really far too much work for me on my own and I didn't have enough money to maintain it anyway. The government was asking for a crippling amount of inheritance tax and our family solicitor said it would be very beneficial to sell the farm before my mother had been dead for three years, because apparently this would lessen the tax burden considerably. Therefore I decided to spend the winter packing up what had been our family home for over forty years. It was a mammoth task because my father had been a terrific hoarder and every shed and barn was absolutely crammed with old bits and pieces! I spent every spare evening going through torn, damp documents, piles of clothes and boxes of old family china and silver etcetera, trying to decide what to do with everything that I found. In the day time I lit huge bonfires with all the rubbish from the various nooks and crannies and made innumerable trips to the local charity shops. It was a real 'clearing out' or, as I now realise, a 'complete cleansing', of the entire property.

While all this was going on, the universe started to make me aware of all sorts of other people who had been involved in my life as a witch/healer. I was able to piece together that the life had taken place towards the latter end of the 'witch trials' in Europe and that I had actually stood on trial. I was introduced in this life to several of the people who had been instrumental in bringing me to trial in the past life and was very surprised to find that most of them had been healers and were healers again in this life! They had apparently used me as a scapegoat because I was more popular with the public than they were and they felt a certain amount of jealousy towards me. They did not like the way I kept myself to myself and just got on with what I wanted to do in my own quiet way. I was never short of clients and they were often struggling to find them. So when the authorities were making noises about catching witches and putting them to death, they banded together and decided to tell whoever was in charge, that I was the undesirable witch they needed to 'get'.

As all this dawned on me, I felt inspired to write down a list of those people who I thought had brought me to trial. As each name was given to me and the list grew, I felt a dark fear and knew that at a deep level I was very afraid of what these people had done to me and what they might do to me again. It was part of the darkness that had always sat deep within me and these latest revelations were forcing me to acknowledge it. There were about nine people on the initial list and as I studied it and thought of each individual in turn, I realised for the first time that I had made a huge mistake. As I had stood on trial, I had been internally blaming THEM for what was happening to me. I thought of Jesus on the cross and how he had said,

"Father, forgive them, for they know not what they do!"

I felt dreadful because I had failed to forgive them and prayed immediately for forgiveness for this omission and begged that they should now be forgiven for wronging me. I knew there was a part of me that had brought this death upon myself because I had failed to get the right balance between serving my family and serving the community. At the same time I knew that I hadn't 'deserved' to be put to death, but then neither had Jesus. My death was the price that some 'sons/ daughters' of God are occasionally asked to pay during an earthly life.

One of the people the universe brought to me at this time was a friend of the tenant who was living temporarily in my mother's house. He had come over to the farm to play tennis with my tenant earlier in the year and I had met him very briefly. Unbeknownst to me he was in quite a mess in his life and he felt that I might be able to help him. As he lived in London I was very dubious about how much help I could actually give him but it turned out that the large distance between us actually gave ME a tremendous gift. He rang me one day, shortly after my return from Egypt, and we chatted on the telephone for quite a long time. I hated the telephone and had always fought against this form of communication, preferring to talk to people in person. I asked him if we could meet and he drove from London to see me which helped a great deal. But after that, because he lived in London and was extremely busy, I had to communicate with him by telephone. As the months went by, I began to realise that there was no other practical way to talk to him and I would have to accept the situation as it was and get on with it. Once

I had stopped fighting myself, I became much more capable on the phone, until I finally stopped worrying about it completely and was then very grateful to him for helping to remove this barrier.

It isn't part of my story to relate much of this man's path or problems but it is important for you to know that he had come into this life feeling totally unable to commit himself in relationships, work or even such things as moving house. I knew this was because he was afraid to be completely truthful in some way. I was shown, by the spirit world, an incredibly complicated 'web' that he had woven for himself, that was sitting directly above his head. It only had one exit route, which was hidden so well that it was going to be extremely difficult to find, but from this I knew that if he could get over his 'truth' hurdle, he would eventually find his way out of his commitment problems. Over the following months, as we talked on the 'phone, he gradually moved towards understanding 'total honesty'. But I heard my guides repeat several times that it was 'easier for a camel to pass through the eye of a needle than for a rich man to reach the kingdom of heaven!' This man's journey was indeed very, very hard.

It was revealed to me at one point that we had known each other very well in my past life as a healer/witch. Roy, as I will call him, was a scribe of some sort, working for himself and living in a small house in a town near to where I lived. Roy and I had got to know each other after my husband had died and we had become very fond of each other. Roy wanted me to go and live with him in his town house as his wife, to care for him and share our future. I was totally committed to my healing and I knew I didn't want to compromise it in any way so I refused to go. So we were loving friends, living apart and I was quite happy with the arrangement.

At the time I was on trial, Roy was questioned about his connection with me. He told the authorities that our association was purely business, partly because he was a little bit angry with me for not committing to him and partly because he knew if he admitted to any other connection with me, his life might be in danger. He had realised the seriousness of my trial and was too afraid to be honest. Although he was believed by the authorities at the time, his friends and clients were disgusted with him. They all knew he had lied and they took their business elsewhere. So Roy survived with his life but he lost everything else.

In this life Roy had obviously recognised his connection with me at some level when he first met me and I certainly knew I had known him before. His inner self must have told him that I held a 'key' to his release, which was why he continually 'phoned me over the next few months, trying to address his severe commitment problems. One day, when he was visiting the farm, I revealed the past life to him. He didn't remember any of it himself but he did have a rapport with the feelings that it had left inside him and he did realise that he and I had a connection beyond this life. I asked him whether, if he could live that life again, he would be brave enough to tell the truth and he replied carefully,

"I hope I would."

I continued to work on the truthfulness aspect of this life in great depth with him until he understood exactly where he was going wrong. When he had first contacted me, he had obviously been at a similar crossroads to when I had been put on trial in his past life, where he was allowing fear to take hold of him and he was struggling to choose honesty above all else. His meeting and continual dialogue with me over the last few months was definitely fulfilling his desire to overcome the block that his lack of bravery in the past life had left him with. I don't know if it was an important part of his healing for me to tell him that I forgave him for what he had done but I did it anyway!

Roy's healing took many more hours of talking on the telephone and a few more visits to the farm. There was one particularly notable visit in which he managed to let go of all his business problems and trust God, extremely bravely, which had an immediate and very beneficial effect on the business matters he was struggling with. This was all part of catapulting him forwards into 'surrendering to the highest' and I really admired the dedication and determination that he showed in which to achieve it. Now, quite some time later, Roy has managed to move his life on very successfully. It has taken a lot of courage on his part, (he squeezed himself through the eye of the needle!) which is a great credit to him. He now has a lovely girl friend and a new born baby. He has managed to move house and his business is completing. He is fifty three years old and, I believe, greatly released from what happened in the past life and the fear it left him with.

I have included Roy's story here because it shows yet another aspect between the two lives that had been unfolding but Roy was not one of the people who ganged up to put me to death. The 'gang' as I shall call it, was gradually revealed to me at about the same time that I went to Egypt and some of its members were quite a shock to me. One of them was my dearest friend who I met at the hotel training course, at eighteen years of age. A possible member was Derek, the acquaintance who had tried to help/hinder my husband and I when we were separating. Two members were healers who I met in quite a strange way when I was searching for a new house. Another was a random lady who had come to stay with me some years ago because she needed some help. Some local healers who I had recently been introduced to, also turned out to be a part of it. There were also a few others who I suspect were involved but I have been given no proof to date.

The brief connection that I had with the two healers when I went to view a house was an extremely unnerving experience but it was the one that revealed to me exactly what 'the gang' was all about. I had just started to look around the area to see if there were any properties on the market that I would like to live in. Meanwhile a friend living in Findhorn had put me in touch with a spiritual friend of hers who lived in my county and who was not very well. She asked if I would be able to pay this lady a visit on her behalf, as she lived too far away to do so herself. I therefore went to visit this friend and during the course of conversation she told me there was a property in a nearby village which had just been done up as a type of healing centre and may be of interest to me. I decided to go and have a look at it on my way home. Upon my arrival at the house, I was met at the door by two women. I felt an immediate rapport with them and knew instantly they were healers. I had a good look around the property, which consisted of an enormous house surrounded by a few acres of its own land. I realised it had been done up most beautifully and I was privileged to hear the story of how it had all come about. I was very sad that the owner (one of the women showing me round) was unable to utilize the property as a healing sanctuary herself because she had put such a huge chunk of her own essence into it. However, she told me that the project had crippled her financially and so she was forced to sell it.

I thought long and hard about buying the property because I had come across it in such an unusual way and it seemed to be such an ideal solution for me. But there was something I didn't really like about its position and deep inside I knew that it wasn't right for me. What seemed so sad and unreal to me was that she had created such an amazing healing centre and it appeared that the universe was not going to use it. I couldn't help wondering why! (It was later sold as a private house.) I met up with one of the healers not long afterwards and she spent some time outlining some of her associated problems. I listened with one ear and in my usual fashion and also picked up what the spirit world was communicating to me about her with the other ear. I was shown her blocks and why she was in a mess and I briefly told her something of what I was picking up. This sort of thing was happening to me fairly regularly by now. She listened and we parted on what I thought were good terms.

I was alone in my house a few days later and I forget now whether she telephoned me or I telephoned her but a most extraordinary thing happened. Whilst on the phone to her, she started to tell me how offended she was by many of the things I had said to her when we had met up. I then felt an enormous tugging and found that the telephone was being pulled away from my ear and was being kept at arms length. I could just about hear what she was saying but there was a strong rush of air keeping the receiver away from me! Then I realised she was accusing me of saying all sorts of things that I hadn't actually said! I was totally bemused! Where on earth had she got all this from? Did she know who she was talking to? What was going on? The phone was continually being forced away from my ear so it was difficult to concentrate completely on what she was saying and I was so confused by it all that I couldn't reply much anyway! I do remember that she ended up by announcing that she would have to think very seriously about whether she was ever going to meet me again.

After the call I felt really dreadful but I couldn't take what she had said very seriously because the universe had shown me so plainly that I really had nothing to worry about. The phone had been kept away from my ear to leave me in no doubt that what she was saying wasn't to concern me too much. I talked it over with a friend the next day and she was convinced that this was a classic case of mirroring. I didn't know what mirroring was at that stage but I learnt very quickly that I had probably 'mirrored' this woman's problems back to her. Somehow her unconscious mind had revealed things to her whilst I had been talking, to the extent that she thought she had heard me say things I hadn't even said, and she had been unable to face everything. This had caused her to throw everything she didn't like hearing back at me and then blame me. I felt I had probably been used as some sort of catalyst by the universe, to try and get a point across.

This experience opened a whole new set of doors for me and I started to learn about mirroring in a big way. In this woman's case though, I knew there was nothing I could do to put her right at that moment, but I did write her a letter saying I was very sorry that I had offended her, and assured her I would never contact her again.

For a long time after this I was very nervous of talking to people in case there was a repetition. Deep down I knew I had nothing to worry about because of what had happened to the telephone receiver and that was obviously why the universe had done it. But I kept thinking that perhaps there was more to the episode than met the eye and so eventually I asked to be shown what it was. As I was laying the fire one morning I was taken into a semi trance state and told that this woman had been one of the people in my life as a witch who had turned me over to the authorities. In fact she had been one of the main healers who had turned against me because she knew I had 'understandings' of spirituality that she did not have and she was somewhat envious. She was also responsible for turning many other healers against me, her influence being very strong in the area. I then became aware that both ladies/healers who had met me at the door when I first went to look at the property were a part of the gang.

I was then shown that seeing me again in this life had resurrected the past life feelings and this had caused her imbalanced thoughts which had culminated in the odd telephone call. She thought she knew exactly who she was as far as healing and spirituality were concerned and I had severely rocked her boat, quite unwittingly! I knew that the universe had caused us to meet, to reveal this to me, so that I could unravel yet more of that wretched past life and pray for her release and growth, which I have done ever since.

And so my first real awareness that there had been a 'gang' against me in that life had begun. I came to realise that a part of my path in this life was to help those involved to be released from what had happened and to aid them on to deeper levels of spirituality, whether by prayer or conversation. I also knew that a lot of the people I would help in the future would not have been a part of that actual gang, indeed I would never have met them before, but my work for them would be similar.

I now recognised that the dark fear that had lain at the depths of me all of this life, that caused me to sob in the bedroom when I was little, calling myself such an awful person, was the same fear that I felt when I thought of this woman. Equally, the fear that had erupted so suddenly after my mother's death was of the same calibre. So I continually handed these feelings to God. Dealing with it all felt way beyond ME!

12

Kate's visit

In November 2005 I felt suddenly inspired to place an advertisement in our local 'Connections' magazine. I would state simply, that I was a healer of some twenty years experience and was available if anyone needed any help. I rang the Connections number to see how to go about putting in an advertisement. The man I spoke to was extremely nice and said his deadline was in an hours' time and if I could fax it to him NOW he would make sure it got into this month's edition. I was surprised into action and thought to myself that the timing of the whole thing was so amazing, it was undoubtedly meant to be done right at this minute! I quickly wrote out what I thought would do and sent off the fax within the hour.

About two hours later, as I was gardening, I thought to myself,

"What on earth have I done? I must be mad!"

I started laughing and feeling really shocked. I knew that if I had not been rushed into action, and had

had time to think the whole thing out, I would never have placed the advertisement! Then of course, some inevitable thoughts followed;

"It must have been meant! The universe definitely intended this advert to go in and found a way of doing it that I could not back out of"

I wondered why and then decided to simply accept that whatever the reason was, I would find out soon enough. I promptly forgot about it and that was that.

One evening, about a week later, a lady called Kate phoned me. I will use her proper name because I don't know who she was, where she came from or even if she really existed! She said she had read my advertisement in Connections and wanted to come and see me. I arranged for her to come over the following Wednesday afternoon, weather permitting.

Wednesday dawned and the ground was completely covered in snow. By about lunchtime I decided I'd better ring her and tell her that the roads around me were still a little bit dodgy but I was unable to get through on the telephone number she had given me. I therefore just had to hope she would be okay. She duly arrived and I led her into the kitchen which was the only warm room in the house. I wondered what she wanted because, as I made her a cup of tea, she kept asking me questions about myself, but I answered politely, as one does! I tried to ask her several times, why she had come to see me but she kept turning the conversation off herself and back onto me. I felt a bit confused but her eyes bored into me in such a compelling fashion that I was rather intimidated. At one stage I felt as if she was looking right into my soul and it was very unnerving. She wanted to know all about my plans and what I was doing with the house. I told her that I was in limbo and wasn't sure what lay ahead. She looked intently at me and said,

"You really don't know, do you?"

Then Kate began to talk. She told me not to worry about her needs today and that she was a very, very, very old soul! She explained how I was currently in a void, how I was just finishing tying up the loose ends of my past life doings and that afterwards, had a job to do. She explained how I was currently being prepared for that special spiritual job in every way. She said all my karma had been resolved and I had nothing more to settle; I was clean! She then went on to tell me that billions of souls were going to move on in the next few years in a type of earth cleansing and that some souls were leaving already. I sat listening to her in complete amazement! Whoever was this person?

Kate asked to have a little look around the outside of the property which of course I allowed and was amused to see how she sniffed the air wherever she went. At one point she turned round to look at me and said,

"You will never, ever see me again!"

I really didn't know how to respond to this statement so I remained silent. She continued her tour while I just followed like a confused lamb. She seemed to know exactly where she wanted to go so I just let her carry on. Eventually she turned back to where her car was parked and said it was time to go. She gave me a hug and said again,

"You will never see me again."

Once more, I didn't reply. I was far too bemused by this time. She got in her car and drove off and all that I had to show for her visit were the tracks that the car had left in the melting snow.

I went back into my house feeling most peculiar. Who ever was this person? Undoubtedly she had come to give me some encouragement and direction and undoubtedly she was a very old soul. Her whole presence shouted it!! Then I began to laugh to myself. Had this really happened? Was she a real person or was she a ghost? Had I been dreaming it all and was I about to wake up? But then I remembered the car tracks and decided she must have been real! I walked around the house in a complete daze for quite a while after that.

But as the hours went by I began to settle internally in an amazing way. I felt quite at ease, knowing I didn't have to worry about my future any more and that it was all taken care of. I felt I could continue living on a day to day basis, following my instincts, allowing my life path to stretch out in front of me. I knew everything would work out just right and that I would be happy soon. I recognised I was being taught many things but fairly gently, thank goodness. I felt as if I had already been through so much pain that gentle was the only way forward at this stage. I knew mum was close, taking care of me but I could also feel angels, one very pure one in particular. And I felt very lucky indeed!

Nobody else rang me from the advertisement which I had put in the Connections magazine, which confirmed to me that it had all happened so I could receive Kate's visit. It was really quite an extraordinary experience!

13

A miracle and a decision

As I CONTINUED THE TASK of cleaning out a home that had been occupied for over forty years by two consecutive generations of my family, I had to refer to all the different members of the family to ascertain what things belonged to whom and who wanted to keep each item. It was a very emotionally draining process which meant I could not do too much at once. I had to travel seriously back down memory lane, some of which was pleasant enough and some of which was rather painful. The whole procedure took me about six months and by the time spring came, the main bulk of it had been done so I could be ready to auction the house at short notice during the summer, if I had to.

At the same time I was busy chasing around the country looking at potential new homes for myself. There were quite a few big properties around but I never felt they were in quite the right location for me. I asked the universe several times to show me which area would be most suitable and I always got the strong instinct that the area in which I already lived was the best. This was fairly odd because I had never really settled at the farm; my friends were mostly in Herefordshire, and a big part of me felt I should move on from my current family home, with its memories and its ties. However as I started to walk around the immediate area looking at local properties, it hit me very strongly that I was meant to stay local! I therefore started to let everyone in the vicinity know what I was looking for and my price range. Around this time I received a very good offer for the farm from an estate agent who had come to value it for probate purposes.

So the winter had passed very busily and as the new spring approached I began to prepare myself mentally for the second summer on my own. Panic was never very far away because I had so much to do and I knew that to maintain the houses, farm and gardens on my own, was a tall order. However, some helpful changes had taken place on the family front. My elder sister and I had been repairing our relationship all winter and were now on much better terms. My husband and I were settling into our new way of life and we saw each other weekly because he needed to come to the farm to oversee the sheep. Our friendship was becoming more manageable and he was becoming calmer over everything that had happened. My younger sister was a massive support to me on the emotional side of things so, although a mammoth task lay ahead, I had a more stable background from which to accomplish it.

Then a most extraordinary set of circumstances occurred in May which altered everything. It started when I went to see a very nice house about half an hour's drive away from the farm. This house was perfect for me in every way. It was situated in a small hamlet in a fairly secluded spot. It was decorated beautifully and had a lovely garden and grounds. As I looked round it I knew I could be very, very happy living in it and would struggle to find anything nicer. For twenty four hours or so I thought very seriously about buying it but there was something intangible holding me back. After much deliberation I realised that, although it was absolutely true that it would be a good place for me to live, I felt as if I would be burying myself alive. I was looking at the type of house I would probably need in ten to fifteen years time, not now!! This was such an eye-opener to me because I started to realise I was not a seventy year old looking for a retirement home but a fifty year old with plenty of life left in me! I was therefore jolted into a serious rethink about what type of property I was looking for.

The second thing that happened was that I went to see Sally, the healer who I had visited many years ago and who had helped me with Edward's nightmares. I had come across the tape she had made during my first visit to her, quite by accident (I thought!) when clearing out a cupboard, and she had luckily written her phone number on it. I listened to the tape and was quite amazed by what was said on it. I realised she had been quite accurate on most of her predictions for my life but it was quite astonishing how much more I understood about what she was saying as I listened to her tape some fifteen years later! She had told me things about myself that I had no idea were true at the time but fifteen years later I knew they were.

Setting off to see her on the Glastonbury Tor, where she now lived, I had absolutely no idea what to expect. My memory of her was of a witch-like figure with long, grey, sticking out hair and that she had been rather frightening. However, seeing her again was just fine! She had her long hair tied back and she looked a great deal more normal than I had expected. And so began a three hour session during which she was very blunt with me but also very kind. She told me how I must be freer from my husband because I was still too much under his influence. She outlined all sorts of possibilities for my future and she confirmed that the universe was now ready and waiting to use me to the full. As she spoke I realised how much I had changed since I last saw her and just how many gifts I now had to share with people. But probably one of the most important parts of our discussions was the bit about the farm. She went into her own trance state and from there told me that I had a choice. I could start up a retreat/sanctuary at the farm where I already lived so people could come and stay and receive healing or I could start up a similar thing somewhere else; the choice was mine! She felt that if I did it at the farm it would happen quickly and if I chose to do it elsewhere it would still happen, but it would take longer.

As I drove home I knew I wanted to do it at the farm. My mother had always hoped her home would be used for healing. Everybody without exception, who visited the farm, enthused about what an amazing place it was, even on a grey November day! The whole ambiance of the place was so suitable for what I wanted to do and I knew I would never find anywhere to better it. I decided then and there that if it was possible, this was what I wanted to do, despite the enormous work load.

Theoretically, of course, it was financially impossible for me to stay at the farm but the 'mountain moving' universe had other ideas! It was now nearly three years since my mother had died and we were approaching the deadline by which the solicitor had advised us to sell the farm. Mum's affairs were by no means sorted out but it wouldn't stop us selling up if we wanted to. However, one sunny May day, not long after I had been to Glastonbury, my older sister received the news that our farm had been accepted for full agricultural property relief, which meant there would be no inheritance tax to pay on the house and the farmlands! This was totally unexpected by our solicitor because there were properties all over the country fighting for just this and not being successful. That our farm should receive the full relief was staggering! As if that were not astonishing enough, we then received word from the relevant governmental department that they would accept an oil painting which my mother had owned, in lieu of inheritance tax. This picture was an exceptionally fine piece of artwork by Edward Lear and had belonged to the family since Edward Lear had first painted it in 1865. It depicted Jerusalem from outside its walls and if you stood in front of it, it felt as if you were actually there. We had been trying to find a museum that would like to display it ever since my father had died but had recently been toying with the idea of selling it because it was impracticable for the three beneficiaries (myself and my two sisters) to own it. The government was now saying that it would accept the picture for an enormous sum of money that we could offset against the rest of the inheritance tax that we owed. It all seemed too good to be true!

At this point my sister realised that there would be almost enough money to balance our mother's estate and that it would be possible for me to remain at the farm. She came straight over to see me, to give me the good news and to impress upon me that I now had a different decision to make. Well, my decision was very quick indeed for although these events had happened within a month, I knew in my heart that I definitely wanted to give the sanctuary a go. My biggest reservation was that I would not be able to manage the farm on my own but I decided to trust that the universe would provide all that I needed.

My entire family was delighted that I decided to stay at the farm. My children were able to retain their home, my husband could visit the place he loved, my sisters could continue to visit their childhood paradise and I could start my new life's purpose! I felt so happy and thanked God, the universe and everything else from the bottom of my heart, for only something divine could have accomplished this miracle!

14

Some unexpected links

THE FARM HAS A SMALL lodge situated at the bottom of the driveway and for some years my mother had a married couple living there, who helped on the farm for two days a week in return for free accommodation. In December 2005 the couple left and the lodge was left empty so I needed to find some more people to help me out, fairly urgently. I thought I would try advertising in a spiritual magazine, hoping I might get some interest from reliable, like-minded people. In fact I had over twenty replies to the advertisement and although I considered quite a few of them might be suitable, took on the first couple I interviewed, who came from London. It was a bit of a risk because they didn't know much about living in the countryside but they had been asking the universe to help them move out of London for two years and I wanted to give them that chance. We all hit it off from the moment we met and they were really excited about living at the farm and helping with my project. We arranged for the wife, Nicky, to help in the house for half a day a week and for her husband Martin, to help on the farm for one and a half days per week. Martin was a superb builder and handyman and he offered to help renovate anything in the house for me if I wanted. The whole arrangement seemed wonderful and we were all very happy with it.

As the first few weeks went by I could hardly believe how close we all were and it wasn't long before I realised that Nicky had been my mother in a previous life. She and I had such an incredibly natural bond and we loved each other, so very dearly. Of course it was no accident that we were together and in a deep trance state one day, a past life that we had lived in together, was revealed to me:

Many centuries ago, Nicky and I had lived in a large town in Egypt. Our house had been small, dark and very modest. Nicky's husband, who may have been my father, had left when I was fairly small and Nicky had brought me up on her own. We had a very close relationship and were very happy. With a shock, I suddenly became aware that this was a life which had already been partially revealed to me and it was when I had been in love with Graham. I was amazed! So Nicky had known Graham! I sat in my trance state, my thoughts swirling like a stormy ocean, with this discovery. My attention was then shifted to Nicky and I was made aware of how she had been feeling in that life. She knew Graham and I would be safe enough in our affair as long as we were discreet. However as time went on she saw how difficult it was becoming for Graham to visit me and she worried because I was so much in love.

On the day I ran from the house to find Graham in

the palace, she had begged me not to go, but I wouldn't listen. She was terrified as I left and followed me at a distance. In my trance state I was then switched to feeling Nicky's distress after I had been taken prisoner. It affected the rest of her life greatly and she was for ever repeating,

"If only she had listened!"

I went out to mow the lawn still in half a trance and as I paced up and down with the mower, hardly noticing what I was doing, I felt so ashamed. I was seeing Nicky's side of the story for the first time and being made aware of just how much I had hurt her. I had been so selfish, never thinking about her and what I was doing to her. I knew if I could go back to that time I would act completely differently and I wished I could put it right. I stopped my mower and prayed at a very deep level,

"Nicky, I would never have knowingly hurt you and I am very sorry that I did not listen to you. I never even registered hearing you calling after me until now! I do hope you can forgive me, I truly am very sorry."

As I came fully out of the trance I wondered if I would ever be able to tell Nicky what I knew!

As it happened I had the opportunity to tell Nicky about a month later. I asked her if she would be interested in hearing a snippet of a past life which I had unearthed and she said she would be fascinated! I started to relate it to her and when I got to the bit about creating a scene outside the palace she suddenly announced,

"I remember that!"

I stared at her in astonishment and she explained, "I suddenly got a flash of memory and I can remember that happening!"

We sat and looked at each other in total amazement! We just knew it was true! A few seconds later, I got a vision of her hanging out very colourful clothes on a clothes line. I didn't know why I should be seeing this but decided to tell Nicky and she immediately started laughing. She said she had always wanted her own clothes line but in London she was unable to have one. When she came to live at the lodge she had the space to have exactly what she wanted – a long outdoor clothes line! We both knew in that instant that this was irrefutable evidence that everything we were thinking was true! I also noticed that she was wearing very colourful clothes! We both felt it was a huge confirmation that she and I were together in the right place at the right time.

After I had finished relating the rest of that past life to Nicky, I told her I felt we had met up again in this life to be together, mostly to have the chance to complete the friendship we had missed out on in the previous life. I asked her if she would forgive me for what I had done and of course she said she would. I knew I had really upset her in that life and I prayed it could be corrected in this life.

After that the friendship between Nicky, Martin and I just grew even stronger. We discussed plans for the farmhouse, plans for the farm and what all the various possibilities were. Martin told me he had already experienced setting up a healing centre a few years ago and all that he had learnt there was proving to be a great help to us.

I decided I would prefer to live in the newly renovated house in which my mother had lived and that we would convert the main farmhouse into accommodation for our future guests. My mother's house was much smaller than the farmhouse and would be easier for me to manage on my own. I decided to ask my tenant, who had rented my mother's house for over a year, if he could start looking for somewhere else to live, but I told him there was no hurry as during the summer I was too busy to move anyway. Meanwhile I started to think about all the changes I could make to the main farmhouse in order to turn it into a retreat/sanctuary/healing house......whatever!

I have to say that whatever we decided to do to make the farmhouse usable was going to be a mammoth task. My father had done all the internal repairs and decorating himself, over the years he had lived in it, but he had done it with very little money. Therefore much of the workmanship was bodged and was not safe enough for guests! Although my husband and I had poured our extra money into the property while we had been in it, it was still a fairly basic affair and certainly nowhere near good enough to be used by visitors. I knew I didn't have enough resources to turn it into a respectable and safe condition so I started talking to Source asking, if I could please have some financial help. I decided to picture an envelope arriving in the post and when I opened it there would be a cheque inside with enough money to do whatever was needed. I pictured this whenever I thought about it. I didn't ask for any more than I needed, I simply asked for the universe to provide what was appropriate!

Martin and I worked hard all summer to complete the farm work, wanting to leave the winter months free to start our project. In September, we decided to build a car park in the grounds of the main garden, ready for any visitors. I was very keen to keep the farm and my house separate from any guest accommodation, mostly because I knew I would need to retain some privacy. I saw this could be done by creating a new entrance off the front driveway and turning the garden door of the main house into the front door. This would give the two houses their own completely separate entrances and allow my family home to be as undisturbed as possible.

A car park might seem a funny place to start a project like this but I didn't question my instinctive desire to begin there. In fact, during those first few weeks, I became increasingly aware that there was a spiritual manager guiding the entire project and that I was simply the receiver of the plans. I didn't feel I had to worry about anything. I just had to listen to my inner guidance and follow it as closely as I could. So, as my instincts told me to start with the car park, we did just that! How I was going to finance it was a little bit worrying but I trusted that it would all would work out and I dug into my own limited savings fund to buy everything we needed. After we had cleared the trees and undergrowth from the area I thought would be suitable, I received guidance to make the car park twice the size. Obviously my ideas had not been big enough! So we duly doubled the size of our clearing, laughing as we did so, wondering what on earth was ahead!

As far as the house was concerned, we decided we could start with the attic because it was only being used for storage. It meant we would not have to rush my tenant out of mum's house before he had found himself another place to rent because I could continue living in the rest of the main house for the time being. We decided to put a little card up in the hall of the main house telling any visitors briefly what was happening and to ask for donations if they felt they would like to support the project. I felt most peculiar about doing this because in the twenty plus years that I had been helping people, I had never asked anyone for any financial reward. But it turned out to be a big learning curve for me because, as I had nowhere near enough money to renovate the house myself, I had to allow myself to open a door to help from other sources. At this point quite a few people were coming to me for different types of support and healing and it was taking up much of my time.

So the project got happily underway. My life seemed to be coming together very nicely and for the first time for a long time I felt I had a real purpose, despite the fact that the blue print was held securely in spiritual hands and I hadn't seen it! My trust that all would be well was never in doubt.

At around this time I had been reading a book which suggested it was possible, just before going to bed, to ask the universe to take you, in your sleeping hours, to a place where your soul could learn and grow. I thought this was an idea worth trying so one night I humbly asked if this would be possible for me. I had no idea what immediate and dramatic results it would have!

At about four o'clock the next morning I woke up after a vivid dream in which I was being told that I was resenting everyone around me. That included spirits, mum, people in the flesh, all sorts! Well, that was news to me! I was very surprised because I had NO idea at a conscious level that I held any resentment at all, so I thought it must be hidden at a very deep level. In my sleepy state I acknowledged the possibility of the concept and the next thing I knew I was experiencing a huge release from it and felt as if I was being healed. I spent the rest of the night saying,

"Thank you!" in a very heartfelt and meaningful way.

I started feeling very calm and relaxed. I also felt it was necessary to stop fretting and worrying about being alone on the farm and to ask only that I should grow spiritually and heal the part of me that felt resentment at such a deep and unknown level.

The next night I awoke again at four o'clock with flashes of knowledge running through my brain. My husband had been over the day before and I remember being shown how I must stand up to him. He has such a strong personality that I tend to let him walk all over me. I was shown that we have problems between us because I ALLOW him to do that. It was nobody's fault but my own and it was up to me to stop it. Other relationships with various different people flashed before me, and I was shown how I allow everyone to walk all over me and it's a big weakness within me. Another flash showed me that I am alone in life at this time so that I have the opportunity to find the strength in myself, to BE myself. Then the life as a witch flashed before me and I knew in that life I had been the opposite. I had been too strong, and my family had suffered because of it. I had obviously put it right in this life but because I was so nervous of making the same mistake again, I had gone too far the other way! I was tossing and turning in the bed as these thoughts popped in and out of my head and I was generally feeling very bothered and uncomfortable. I asked if I could have some help in balancing myself out. Then an extraordinary thing happened, I heard a voice saying,

"Feel the pain and the emotion, go into it!"

And as I lay in bed I obeyed, at least twice, and it was awful.

I spent the rest of the night mulling all this over, sleep being far from the most important issue by now. I knew that somehow I must gain in personal strength and be much tougher emotionally too. I knew I must find the courage to face up to people. I realised that I was like this because of trying to rectify the previous life but I yearned for the balance between the two ways of being and I prayed fervently for help. And in the silence of the night I heard the clock tick, ticking by my bed, as I struggled with all these thoughts.

I must have drifted off to sleep again however, because the next thing I became aware of was a whole lot of fingers pointing rudely towards me. I knew instantly that I was back in the previous life, and I heard people shouting at me,

"YOU DID THIS, YOU, YOU, YOU!"

I saw and felt fingers stabbing into me. Then I was told,

"You are allowing this! You are allowing them to point their fingers at you."

I jolted myself upright in my bed and cried in anguish,

"I'm going to turn those fingers around, for they are damaging me!"

And I knew in that moment that I must achieve this if I was to progress further.

So my asking to be taken to a place where my soul could learn and grow had produced very dramatic results! Little did I know that this was part of the run up to a very painful set of events that were to follow, but at the same time I was treading a path that was 'MEANT TO HAPPEN.'

15

Learning about
spiritual journeys

JUST AS ALL THE FARMHOUSE plans were taking off and
we had begun pulling things apart in the attic, my elder
sister was taken very ill. She was rushed into hospital
in the middle of the night because she had an ovarian
cyst that had burst and she had to be operated on
immediately. She needed to have a full hysterectomy
because it turned out that the cyst was malignant and
she was diagnosed with ovarian cancer. This was a
terrific shock to us all because we were not expecting
yet another huge family problem.

My younger sister was living in Bristol and was fully
occupied looking after two young children so I knew
I would have to drop everything that I was doing and
look after my elder sister myself. I was more than happy
to do this realising that the farmhouse project would
just have to wait!

It turned out to be a time of enormous revelations

for both my sister and myself. The shock of discovering she had cancer at fifty three years of age, catapulted my sister into looking at herself in depth and she decided to work out exactly why it had happened or she might well die. She realised reasonably quickly that she had contracted cancer because of things she was doing to herself and she knew the remedy lay in herself too.

The next few weeks were unbelievably taxing for us both. All her life I had offered to help my sister because she was bulimic and all she had ever said was,

"I'm not ready!"

But this time, when I said to her,

"You're going to have to accept help now" she said,

"Yes! I know"

She felt totally overwhelmed by her condition and very, very frightened. I was pretty frightened myself because it is never easy to 'tune in' accurately and help a member of your own family, when you're in a bit of a panic. On the first night she was staying with me, after I had picked her up from hospital, I was snuggling down into my bed when I was suddenly filled with an absolutely beautiful peace. I heard a voice saying to me,

"You won't have to do anything! Don't even think about how to help her, just empty yourself and let yourself BE. All that you need to say will be revealed in its own good time!"

I felt so tremendously relieved! Nothing depended on me; it was all going to be okay. I was incredibly thankful.

There was actually nothing easy about my sister's subsequent journey. She had to strip herself bare and be one hundred per cent honest with herself and with me, to achieve any results. I was forced to give her some home truths which I absolutely hated doing (and she hated receiving) and if I hadn't known that the spirit world was in charge, I might not have had the courage to do it. Yet at the same time I marvelled at how the universal plan led us smoothly from one conversation to another. People called at the house at exactly the right moment, books turned up on cue and the telephone calls and my promptings all gelled beautifully. Things came to a head one morning when I realised that the only way forward was for her to give her life to God. We had beaten about the bush long enough and it was clear this was her path. I told her what I felt but discovered I was only confirming what she already knew and she was already looking to do it. And all the time she was struggling with her inner world, my poor sister was also trying to recover from her major operation!

Through our painful talks, my sister and I came to realise a huge amount of our problems originated from our parents. We had always known our father was very difficult but at this time we had to face the fact that our mother had also unwittingly caused us quite a lot of problems. This all came to light because for the first time in our lives, we were forced to talk deeply to each other about hurtful matters and subsequently unearthed many wounds that had lain dormant for a long time. It is not my intention here to relate much of my sister's story, but to simply tell you that because of her extremely honest approach to our discussions, she was able to begin unravelling her problems very quickly. I had helped so many people in the past but as the days went by, I knew that my sister was one of the most honest people that I had ever come across and I admired her courage enormously. She went through hell in those weeks. She hated me at times, and loved me at others, but she never flinched from what she had to do. And as the weeks went by we found the answers, and she found God.

One of the trickier matters I had to bring up with her was her brief association with me in the fateful past life. I told her she had been the soldier who had stopped another soldier from helping me when I was about to be burnt at the stake but at this stage I did not tell her it was Graham. She found it quite disconcerting to find out she had been involved in my past life, particularly as she had no knowledge about that sort of thing. She appeared to accept what I was saying and was able to apologise to me. She felt quite a connection with it because she had been in the Army for twenty five years in her present life and felt it was conceivable to have had many previous lives as a soldier. At a much later date I told her that it had been Graham with whom she had fought and that was why she had such an instant dislike of him when they had first met. That made a lot of sense to her and we both marvelled at how our past lives can affect so much in this life, whether we recognise it or not! I asked her if she could now bring herself to see Graham in a better light and she said she would try.

The revelations that I received for myself were not as uncomfortable as my sister's because our sessions were predominantly aimed at helping her. But many of the things that we unearthed had a rebound affect on me and certainly caused me much thought. I decided to try and find a transpersonal psychotherapist to help me unravel a few of my own issues. I found a local lady who asked me how many sessions I wanted to book and I felt guided to ask for four. These four sessions were packed with revelations and healing for me. Through her I realised that ever since my abortion, I had never ceased to feel guilty about becoming pregnant and letting my family down. I told her how I had fully made up for it and that mum had agreed that I had, but this clever lady made me realise that there was another side to the story and that my parents had also been at fault. Now I had already seen big time, how my parents had let my sister down but I had never thought for a moment that they had also let ME down. She gently pointed out to me how they had made me feel terrible for becoming pregnant and if they had simply loved me and accepted my situation without judgment, I would not have needed to go looking elsewhere for the love I wasn't being given. This took a while to sink in, because I found it so difficult to believe that my parents could be wrong about anything. Weren't they my PARENTS!! Weren't they always right? I had believed it was all my fault for so long that I struggled to take in what she was suggesting. But, eventually, after I had used up several boxes of her kleenex tissues, I accepted that their attitude to my pregnancy had brought about much of what had happened to me in the following years. We also discussed, however, how my parents had actually acted in a way that they sincerely believed was in my highest interests and indeed, all my life, they had always tried to do what they thought was best for me.

After the second session my therapist asked me to

write down any dreams that I had during the following week. Surprisingly, I had a dream every night and I duly wrote them down. I even had two dreams one night! During the next session I read out what I thought was a completely random collection of non-sensical stories but to my astonishment she interpreted them in the order in which I had dreamt them and produced a whole set of meanings from them. Basically the dreams gave insights into what had happened to me in the past, what was happening in the present and a little of the future too. Dreams took on a whole new meaning for me after that and I have been able to interpret my own and other people's dreams, ever since. I feel she opened up a real gift for me and the spirit world has often communicated to me through dreams since then.

As my sister's health improved and she became stronger, she was able to move back to her own home and take care of herself. We talked on the telephone regularly and each time I knew that I was still being guided in what to say to her and never once worried about it. The entire experience had been such a big learning curve for me. I had been so privileged to help someone on such an important personal journey and I also knew that 'journeys' would play a big part in what I would do in the future. My sisters' experience had given me an invaluable opportunity to grow and expand my understanding of this type of spiritual knowledge. After my sister had left my house, a number of other people who needed help on their life path came to see me and my knowledge increased even more.

Another huge part of this experience was how my sister's relationship with God altered. Although had developed a faith very slowly during her life it had not had a major impact on the way she had lived. She now realised that she must listen to the higher power which she had acknowledged, but not trusted before. She relinquished herself to Him fully and was learning to understand exactly what this meant. Being brought to her knees by cancer had shaken her into realising that she could no longer continue to manage her life as she had been and that a major change was called for! I watched her transformation with awe, knowing that now she had given herself into God's hands, her path to total recovery was secure and she would always be looked after.

One year after my sister's operation, she was given the 'all clear' from the doctors and we both feel she will never have to worry about cancer again. She is no longer bulimic and as the root cause has been well and truly exposed and dealt with, I do not feel it will ever cause a problem again. She continues to grow in love and light; her divine wisdom grows ever more clear and she is now a complete joy to be with.

"Thank you mum, for all that you helped to reveal to us in those long and painful days!"

I had felt mum's presence strongly whilst my sister and I were together and I fully believe she wanted us to recognise her faults so that we could become whole people and move on in our lives. My sister and I were too ready to put her on a pedestal while she was alive and no-one sits well on one of those! Once we saw her as a normal human being and had a more balanced outlook on our childhoods, we could see ourselves in a truer light and thus become greatly healed.

16

The universe at work and
more on the 'gang'

Whilst my sister's illness did hold up proceedings on the house for a while, Martin never stopped working hard in the attic, pulling it apart and reshaping it ready for decorating. His enthusiasm for what we were doing was infectious and I soon picked up the reins again after my sister had left my care. I was still picturing opening the post and receiving a cheque whenever I remembered and already a few chunky donations had been left in my donation box in the hall! At the beginning of December my tenant found himself somewhere else to live and it appeared he would be out of my mother's house by Christmas, so it looked as though we could begin a few alterations to the main house, soon after the beginning of the New Year.

Then one day, I received a letter that completely altered the time scale of the whole project. I will not disclose the source but I was being offered a good sum of money specifically towards the main house renovations. I couldn't believe my eyes at first. It didn't come in the form of the cheque that I had pictured! But it was a bigger amount than I could ever have imagined, being promised in writing from two very reliable people. This money would enable us to do all sorts of things to the house that had hitherto been beyond us and to do them in a much nicer way. I raced down to the lodge to share the news with Martin and Nicky and at once we started to make plans excitedly. I must say that it was several weeks before I calmed down enough to think logically over it, but the most important aspect for me at the time, was how the money proved to us that the universe was right behind what we were doing and that we were following our instincts correctly!

A few weeks later the promised money arrived. By this time we had obtained some quotes from painters, plumbers and electricians, to get an idea how far the money would go. It dawned on me that, because of the donation, the whole project would be finished far quicker than I had envisaged when I had first had the idea, and that was obviously part of the divine plan. Most of the time I felt as if I was being manoeuvred anyway because everything seemed to happen so smoothly and in such perfect timing. I just seemed to be prompted as to what to do and when - it was a lovely experience and so stress free!

My husband and sisters were very supportive of all that I was doing for which I was extremely grateful. The children were also right behind the project; my younger son in particular stated how he wanted to be a part of what was going on. There was a definite change in the air around the farm as my tenant moved out and I prepared to move into my mother's house. Furniture was being shifted which hadn't been moved for over forty years and as it moved we almost felt the house sigh and its spirits lift! And by February 2007 the renovations had begun in earnest.

You may have noticed that I hardly ever mention my older son but he had actually played a different role to everyone else in the family. As far as I knew he was not a part of my past life as a witch/healer and had come into our family in this life because he wanted to learn and observe what we were doing. The affect on him has been enormous and the 'cold water baptism' that he received a the age of four has had a positive influence on his life that I have observed many times throughout the years. At some level he is a devout Christian and though he makes his fair share of mistakes in life, his basic beliefs are as secure as they could be. His soul is on a continual search for the truth and, as far as he is able, he is learning to find honesty in every situation. He and I have known each other in other lives but they have no bearing that I have been made aware of, on the story that I am divulging in this book.

Since we had split up, I had been learning a lot about my husband's and my relationship too. While we were together, everything was so on top of me that I could not see the wood for the trees. But once we had been apart for a while, I was able to get a truer perspective on what our real relationship was. It was literally only about five months after we split that I began to realise that I loved him after all! As the months have carried on, that love has been able to deepen and blossom until

I can say in all honesty, that he is one of the best friends I have ever had and I love him very dearly. We see each other fairly regularly and I trust him beyond anyone else. He has had a lot to put up with from me and I am so thankful that he has not turned his back on me.

But one problem that didn't seem to go away, much to my annoyance, was the continual difficulties surrounding the acquaintance who caused the trouble when my husband and I were splitting up. He, Derek, had never been able to stay out of our affairs for long and I now found myself trying to avoid him whenever possible. I detected a peculiar jealousy that he seemed to have about us or at any rate, his feelings towards us were not healthy. I often felt a dense black energy around him and at first I tried to find out why I could feel it but then I gave up because whatever I uncovered, it didn't seem to get rid of it. However I was still fairly certain that he may have been one of the 'gang' in my last life and for that reason, I was very wary indeed.

More news of the 'gang' came to light at around the time I was moving house. I have mentioned periodically my dear friend from my hotel catering days. Well, over the years our friendship had been deepening and although we were leading completely different lives we were both on a spiritual path. She had a spate of looking into all sorts of alternative therapies and I watched from a distance as she picked them up enthusiastically for a while and then moved on to something else. I often felt as if she must know every single alternative practitioner in the south of England and at times I was quite envious of her connections.

A few years ago our journeys started to role closer and we began to communicate on a more level playing field. It didn't matter at all that our paths had been so diverse, we were both broad minded enough to bridge the differences and learn much from each other. She was one of the very few people that the universe allowed me to share things with and I was extremely grateful that she was happy to talk things over, every so often. It was therefore with real horror that I became aware she was one of the gang. I didn't say anything to her when I first found out but the thought was always at the back of my mind when I was with her. I actually couldn't quite understand it because we got on so well and I thought I would probably never need to mention it to her.

Ever since our children were small we have met up once a year for lunch and quite often we have walked the dogs beforehand. November 2006 was no exception and we decided to meet in Witney, half way between her house and mine. As we set off with the dogs she was telling me about some problems she was having with her shoulder and how, whatever she tried, she couldn't overcome it. She had visited many of her usual therapists but no-one had been able to help. As I was listening and walking along I wondered if it had anything to do with our past life connection and for the next mile or so I toyed with the idea of telling her what I knew. My heart was pounding even with the THOUGHT of telling her, let alone actually telling her. I felt she might turn against me. I could lose her friendship. I might never see her again! My thoughts churned and churned until eventually I decided that I must at least try and overcome something of this terrible fear, connected to the gang and trust that the highest good would prevail. My arm pits were literally pouring sweat as I faced a bit of reality here!

So, gingerly, I suggested to her that we may have had a past life together that wasn't particularly pleasing and that it might have a bearing on her shoulder. From her demeanour, I don't think she was expecting this, so I said that if she would like me to, then maybe I could try and outline it for her but I made it clear that I was very nervous about it. She eventually said that it was up to me really and she would listen if I wanted to tell her. I remember taking quite a while before plucking up the extra courage that I needed to carry on. I was just praying all the time that whatever came out of my lips would be from the highest source and for our highest good.

So I began hesitantly and after a few sentences I felt completely taken over by the spirit world. I sank into a deep trance state, so much so, that at every stile we came to, I told her where we needed to go without even looking at the map. We had neither of us walked along those footpaths before but we were lead unerringly, while we conversed deeply. She already knew about some of the past life but she did not know anything about the gang. I told her what I knew about certain members of the gang and how they were appearing in this life in all sorts of guises. I related the story of the healers in the house that I went to visit, and of how the subsequent telephone conversation often came back into my thoughts and I found myself praying for them regularly. I told her of the fear that surrounded the thought of all the gang members and how I felt some part of this life path was to release and heal all that had happened in that life. I said that I felt these people would be helped to a higher level of understanding in the next few years! I knew we had all arranged to incarnate together in this life but I felt very 'attacked' by them so far. The very thought of the 'gang' sent a wave of fear through me, probably because they had all sent me to my death.

My dear friend listened patiently as I said all these things and much more besides and I think she may have guessed that she was connected in some way. I eventually plucked up the courage to tell her how I thought she had been one of them but that she had only been a gang member because she was too scared to stand against the strength of the mob! She had been roped in to make up the numbers and although she had certainly been a part of it, it was unwillingly, because she really had nothing against me.

Whew! It was out! The unsayable was said! I waited with baited breath to see what her reaction would be. To my surprise and enormous relief there was complete calm in the air and instead of experiencing something frightening, she was saying,

"That explains a lot about how I am now and the hang-ups I have in this life!"

I hardly dared to hear her! Could this be true? Was she having a positive reaction to my confession? She seemed to be relieved in some way and said that now she could understand certain things about herself. And as the walk progressed, we talked and talked and talked. When we got to the pub for lunch we hardly paused for breath as in my trance state the conversation was completely 'led'. New doors and understandings were being opened for her, bit by bit, and I was filled with awe at how it happened! I stayed in a fairly deep trance state for most of the time and the conversation was guided from a deep, deep source.

As we walked back to our cars after lunch, I started to 'come round' so to speak, from my trance state and I felt exhausted! But I knew a great thing had happened and that the start of the 'gang' healing had begun. I knew my friend would be able to progress massively after this and her path would grow to a far deeper level than she had been aware of before, and it was partly for this purpose that we had come together in this life. I also realised with trepidation that she had been the easiest member of the gang to approach and that the remainder of the task may not be so easy!

I have watched my friend move on with terrific bravery since then. She is reaching for the very essence of her being and although it isn't coming easily, she never flinches from the task. It is what she wants and she is a great soul. We talk regularly and I am often used to prompt her when she is stuck. She knows this and accepts it and I thank God that we have been so privileged to have been shown how past lives and present lives are linked so inextricably and how, when we recognise it, we can bring about such amazing healing! Her shoulder hardly troubles her now, giving further proof of her release.

17

I find out who I am

As I strolled slowly through the woods one afternoon, slowly, because a snails pace was all I could manage five weeks on from my operation, I was feeling very joyful. I could see the end of the book approaching and therefore the end of my seclusion. It had been a real struggle to sit at the computer and type the words that were pouring out of me on a daily basis, but the words had been flowing constantly since my discharge from hospital and I had been unable to do anything but write them down. This would be an exhausting process at the best of times but in a physically weakened state it had taken even more effort. However the universe knows exactly what it is doing because it knows full well that when I am back to strength I will need to be busy on the farm whereas at this stage I could be kept in a semi trance state, writing a story that was itching to be told. I had felt no inclination to speak to anyone during this period, nor to go anywhere or do anything to the house project. But I knew I would be glad to finish the book, and pick up the reins of my life again, whatever that entailed!

But to continue..................

Just before Christmas 2006, I received the details of some spiritual holidays taking place in the following year, one of which was to Sedona, in Arizona. I felt attracted to this holiday for some reason but as all my money was going into the renovation of the house at this point I didn't give it much serious thought. However, no sooner had the donation arrived, I remembered the holiday again and realised that now my own money had been freed up, a trip abroad was a possibility! It definitely felt right to go to Sedona so I decided to book it up there and then, and hope for the best. It didn't take place until the following May anyway, so I had plenty of time to get organised.

Meanwhile I moved into my mother's house and real work began on the main farmhouse. Now that it was empty we could see just how much had to be done but it soon turned out I had absolutely no need to worry. We found a delightful painter who agreed to paint the whole house for us over the next few months. I had some trouble with the plumbing and plumbers but that was because Martin and I had lessons to learn! We ended up getting a completely new plumber half way through but there was no doubt that this happened for a good reason. He needed a lot of help! In fact most people we hired came because they had something to learn and we, in turn, had things to learn from them. People started to offer furniture and books which they didn't want and invaluable help arrived in all sorts of ways, wherever there was a need. Martin was spending all his hours doing various building alterations in different parts of the house and my own days were extremely full and challenging!

By the time the holiday in Sedona came up I was so busy preparing for leaving the farm for a week that I honestly hadn't thought much about the actual trip! It was only when I got on the aeroplane that I suddenly realised I didn't even know whereabouts in the United States Arizona was! I asked my travelling companion how long the flight was and when she said eleven hours, I realised I was travelling much further than I had bargained for. I got out the map that was in the little pocket of the seat in front of me and started to acquaint myself with some facts! As I stared at the map, I realised with a shock how I had booked to come on this holiday on the pure instinct that this was what I was supposed to do, and had made no other investigations at all!

However, it was absolutely right that I should visit Sedona, land of the amazing vortexes, and what I learnt and experienced there was truly beyond my wildest expectations. In case you are wondering what I mean by a vortex, the native Sedonians describe it as a giant magnet of energy that is natural to mother earth. There are many of these around the world but what makes Sedona so different is that there are between fifteen and twenty vortexes within a five mile radius of each other and each is more powerful than the pyramids in Egypt. There are dousers around who like to measure this natural energy, but for me it was enough to feel the ebb and flow of the massive electrical charge as I climbed each one, receiving revelations as I went.

My travelling companions were all female and absolutely delightful. Our first few nights were spent in a big hotel which had been built on top of a vortex so you can imagine just how powerful it was to stay there. I spent every night having masses of revelations and very little sleep but I didn't mind at all because it was so fascinating. During the day we travelled all over the area from vortex to vortex, some of which were in their natural state and some of which had buildings on them, and our experiences were all wonderful and fulfilling. I learnt a great deal about the American Indians, their symbols and their customs, of which I had known very little beforehand. I think the universe wanted me to gain a better understanding of the qualities which the land, (mother earth) gives us all, of which I had not had the opportunity or inclination to learn before. In fact, my holiday was almost a crash course in opening up to the power of the stones, the plants, the animals, the stars, the desert, and ancient civilisations. We were given the opportunity to use each natural element for ourselves and for the first time in my life I felt the energy in stones, had real communication with a juniper tree, experienced the Native American way of using animal power and wisdom and much, much more. I knew I would be a better and more rounded person with the knowledge I was gaining and able to relate to a wider spectrum of people in the future.

One night we were taken out into the desert to experience a vision quest. I didn't really feel particularly inclined to do this but I must say, some useful things came from it. We were taught how to construct a medicine wheel and then we had to build one of our own in the desert and spend the night, on our own, sitting in the middle of it. I'm afraid I was rather naughty and simply climbed into my sleeping bag, and asked the universe to make sure I learnt whatever it was that I was supposed to learn from the experience and then dropped off to sleep! The others were very good and stayed awake most of the night experiencing glorious views of the stars and having some lovely revelations.

The following morning we all sat round in a circle and before we compared notes on our experiences the night before, the American Indian lady who was leading us, sent us into a meditation. Mine was fascinating and I found out that whilst I had been asleep in the desert a powerful white light had been beaming down on me with great intensity from what seemed like another galaxy! She asked us to look around and see who our guide had been. In my meditative state I found myself looking upwards and suddenly I knew that my guide had been Jesus, or a powerful source of Jesus energy! I was rather stunned by this because I had never before felt quite such a personal connection! I decided not to mention it to anyone in case they thought I was being big headed and indeed a part of me doubted that it was true anyway! Our leader then asked us what name we would give ourselves and I immediately thought, 'Unlabelled.' She then asked us what noise we would make and I knew that I would make a noise like the wind, silent but powerful.

In discussion afterwards I think our leader was quite surprised at what I had to say about my vision quest and my meditation, even though I omitted the Jesus bit. She didn't comment much but the experience taught me a lot about myself and was a fore runner to what was coming on the last day of the holiday. However, one more important thing to relate at this point was that on that same day, we were each taken aside and given a type of American Indian reading. Amongst other things, I was told that I had finished my karma and that I was about to embark on some work for the universe. The interesting thing about this was that this American Indian lady knew nothing about me, but she was telling me precisely what I had been told by Kate on her strange visit and it confirmed to me again exactly where I was in my life.

We spent an extremely interesting day amongst the Hopi Indian tribes, and were taken to one of their villages to look around. We learnt a great deal about their modern life and I could see enviable parts and I could see sad parts. I felt they were just like us really, just another aspect of civilisation to be learnt from! Their reserve was barren for the most part but they managed to grow enough crops for their needs and seemed, by and large, to be content with their lot.

We spent one complete day on a visit to the Grand Canyon, and like millions of people before us, the experience we had was mind blowing. The vastness of it all brought a sense of humbleness to us and a whole new respect for nature. As I sat in a quiet spot overlooking a section of the canyon, I was privileged to be taken into a trance state and shown the canyon as it used to be many thousands of years ago. The landscape was much greener and the canyon was less deep with banks that sloped gradually towards the river at the bottom. The peacefulness was the same but the vastness wasn't quite so spectacular. I didn't know how many years I was looking back but I felt very lucky to have had the experience.

The final day of our holiday dawned and our leader offered to take us to an old volcano that had erupted nine hundred years previously, explaining how it had a magical atmosphere and people often had major revelations there. It certainly was an astoundingly peaceful spot and as we approached it, I felt it was worth coming on the holiday just for this experience! The sun was shining and the whole place was reasonably deserted as we embarked from our bus and set off towards the large expanse of black lava ahead of us. Even though so many years had gone by since it had erupted there was very little vegetation growing; a few old trees and some greenery in little patches but that was all.

The leader put us into a quiet meditative state and then said to us that we could have an hour to wander around on our own before going back to the bus. I set off down the track thinking that I had received so many revelations already, that I really didn't mind if I didn't have any more. I admired the scenery and enjoyed the peace and as I strolled, I seemed to pass all the other group members who were enjoying their own experiences. I was just thinking that I was going to go all the way round without anything unusual happening when I became aware of the sensation of blood on me! I thought that was odd because there was no blood on me that I could see. I walked on towards a round-topped hill covered solely in black lava and as I approached it I was shown three crosses on it. I stopped dead in my tracks for I knew that I was seeing Calvary! I marvelled at this and wondered why I was seeing it. I sat down at the foot of the hill, a little way off the path so that I wouldn't be disturbed by passers by. And as I sat there in the sun, I knew without a shadow of doubt that I had been present at Jesus' death and had sat at the foot of Calvary just as I was now. I was very surprised because never before had I ever suspected living during Jesus' time. Falling fast into a deep trance state, I became aware that I had known Jesus personally and been one of the crowd that followed Him during his life but had not been anyone particularly special. In the distance I saw a troop of Roman soldiers carrying spears, making their way towards me, asking everyone they passed if they had known Jesus. When they came to me they asked me the same question. I said,

"No, I didn't know him!"

I came back to the present with a jolt. Oh no! I had denied him! I, me, this so called follower of truth, had denied him. I sat there in complete shock and disbelief. WHAT HAD I DONE! JUST WHAT HAD I DONE! The realisation was terrible. Feeling absolutely miserable I looked back up the hill. If I had said I had known him, I would have been crucified on a cross beside him. If ANYONE had said they had known him they would have been crucified with him. But there were no other crosses up there except those of the two robbers. That meant quite literally that everyone had denied him, even his nearest and dearest! I sat quietly trying to take all this in, unaware of anything else going on around me. I HATED the fact I had denied him. I was devastated that I had, totally devastated.

Eventually I got up and resumed my walk, plodding slowly along the path, completely absorbed by my thoughts. The path wound upwards and as I reached the top, I found myself with my Calvary hill on one side of me and a beautiful view of a wooded hill on the other. I leant against some wooden fencing, gazing abstractedly at the view, Calvary behind me. Suddenly I realised why I had been put to death in that horrible, fateful witch's life! It was my karma! Nothing else would or ever could, repay what I had done, except my life! As I took this in, there was a certain amount of relief that I had actually paid back my karma and that I had atoned for my despicable denial. My thoughts then jumped to the 'gang'. Thank goodness for the gang! They had me put to death for their own reasons but in doing so, they had allowed me to repay my karma. For the first time in my life I found myself thanking them. Yes! Actually thanking them! What a turn up!

I felt the warm, spring sun on me and became aware of the wooded view again. I was just thinking that I must go back to the bus when I heard a voice in my head saying,

"Ascended master!"

I immediately knew this to mean that I either had been, was or would be, an ascended master! Whatever, I recognised that I was an old, old soul. I also knew in that moment, that I had volunteered to come back to earth in this life but had not needed to for my own salvation. I had volunteered to do a service for the world in which I had lived so many lives; I had nearly completed the first part and the second part was about to begin. But at the same time, I realised that by coming back to earth this time I had given myself the opportunity to grow faster than if I had remained in the spiritual realms.

Yet in amongst all these seemingly grandiose thoughts, I knew I was just a baby. Above me, I could see many ascended masters including the Buddha, Merlin and Jesus, sitting comfortably around a table. Below me, I was aware of the realm that I had lived in for hundreds, possibly thousands, of years! I could look up at the ascended masters from beneath their table; I felt I was crawling amongst their feet, which was where I belonged at that moment, and that I knew nothing of this new realm of spirituality which I had moved into awareness of...............but I HAD closed the door firmly on the old realm.................and in the future, I knew I would have many new and different things to learn!

These revelations were too much to absorb all at once and I returned to the bus in a complete daze, having kept the whole group waiting, but no-one seemed to mind. I sat in silence, in total awe of all that had been revealed, and so incredibly thankful to that amazing volcanic crater!

18

More clarification of my 'Unlabelled' path

I DISCOVERED THAT MY CONNECTION with nature had altered somewhat on my return from Sedona and I began to communicate in a more personal way with what was growing in my garden. One day I specifically remember lying down beneath two majestic trees that are situated on the lawn just outside the big farmhouse. One is a Cedar of Lebanon and the other is a Copper Beech. I lay on the grass, staring up into the branches, wondering what knowledge they would share with me if they had the chance. And as I lay there, in the stillness, I became aware that these two trees were older than most of the out buildings on the farm, and had planted themselves there specifically to draw healing energy to the farm. I identified closely with their greatness and wisdom and felt so humble as I realised that the project I was about to embark on had been thought of long before I had been born, long before even my great grandparents had been born. In fact, it started to evolve when the trees were first planted! It was no accident that two such amazing trees were planted right at the entrance to my sanctuary, and I was suddenly, acutely aware that I was definitely not alone on this project. It was far bigger than me and far bigger than I could imagine! And as I lay, I gave thanks for the knowledge they had shared with me and I revelled in the new relationship that I had with my two new friends.

Another fairly major change at this point was that I was guided to steer clear of reading any books. I was quite frustrated by this as I loved reading and learning from what I read. Wondering if I had heard my guidance correctly I asked God why I was unable to read. I was told that what I had to learn next was not written anywhere and that I must learn to look only inwards for my tuition. This proved to be very difficult at first but as the months went on, I could see the purpose behind it and I tried to stop fighting it. I was, after all, only fighting a habit.

The summer of 2007 was the busiest summer I have ever had. Not only was the farm and garden very demanding but the universe was accelerating progress in the house at an astonishing rate. I could hardly believe how I was managing to keep on top of the various projects and people kept commenting to me on how quickly it was all happening! I did wonder why it was going so fast but as I wasn't in the driving seat, I just accepted it and carried on!

Even more astonishing was the fact that people kept ringing up to ask if they could come and stay. I would tell them we weren't open but it didn't deter them, they wanted to come and live amongst the paint pots and turmoil for a few days! I knew the experience of having these people would give me a better understanding of what I would have to cope with in the future so I allowed most of them to come. It was very difficult trying to find a clean space for them at times, but we managed to complete one bedroom and its bathroom and found just enough furniture and bedding to equip it. The guests mostly came and used the kitchen in my house as the farmhouse one wasn't ready and this had a two fold learning curve for me. Firstly, I lost my private space and having strangers in the house regularly, impinged on my family too much, but secondly, it had hugely benefited the person staying, because their access to me was so increased. I realised that people were booking in naturally, for the amount of time they needed to be at the farm and that the best results were achieved by just allowing conversation to flow, as and when we met. Some wonderful life path accelerations took place and I began to see how God was going to work through me. Just as I had learnt when helping my sister through her hysterectomy, I didn't have to DO anything. I simply opened myself up as a channel and allowed whatever or whoever to do their bit through me, with some amazing results! I prayed only and consistently for the highest good to prevail for all. The outcome of these experimental visitors meant that I would have to find some way of maintaining a balance between allowing the visitors more access to me and yet retaining my family's privacy.

One day my husband and I were in a second hand furniture sale room when my husband pointed out a large picture which depicted Jesus with Jerusalem in the back ground. I looked at it and felt it would sit beautifully on the main wall in the sitting room of the farmhouse. Upon enquiry, we discovered that the picture had only come in late the day before, which startled me because we had originally planned to visit the sale room on the morning of the day before, and if we had, we wouldn't have seen it. I felt the timing of it all was very providential so I decided to buy it.

When I got home I put the picture against the wall that I had imagined it would hang on and I became a little doubtful. Would my guests think that I was a Jesus fanatic and be put off staying at the house? I was very anxious to be 'unlabelled' and putting Jesus up in such a prominent position could be interpreted wrongly. I started looking for other places to hang the picture and generally felt quite uncomfortable about it. Meanwhile, a friend who had spent the week in Sedona with me came to stay, and was very keen to look around the house and give her input to what was evolving. She walked into the sitting room, saw the picture and her jaw dropped. After a pregnant pause she said to me,

"I don't think that picture is a very good idea because it will give people the wrong impression. There will be lots of people like me coming and they won't want to feel this is a church of some sort."

She was voicing exactly what I had feared!

I pondered her reaction to the picture for some hours and felt that there was probably a little bit more than met the eye, to what she had said. A little later I said to her,

"Why did you have such a strong reaction to the picture? What upsets you so much about Jesus?"

First of all she stated that it was purely because she didn't think I should make such a big statement about Christianity when I actually encompass ALL the religions of the world in my being. Well I had to agree that I was doubtful myself, but as we talked further, I knew that there was more to it than that. I found myself going into a mild trance state, seeing her in one of her past lives where she had been running, running, running! There were a lot of people running with her, it was black all around them, and I suddenly realised they were all running from persecution. I felt it was possibly in the days of the Cathars and she had been an ardent follower of Christ at that time. She had managed to escape but the whole event had been very traumatic and a lot of her friends had not escaped and had lost their lives. I knew the fear that had accompanied this event had often resurfaced in this life and she had felt it again, when she had first seen the picture.

I told my friend what I had picked up and she nodded her head. She admitted to me that she had several dreams some years ago when she had experienced 'being pursued and persecution' and that what I had said made complete sense to her. We discussed the possibility of her letting the fear go and acknowledging Jesus again. I suggested that perhaps she had been wrong to run in that life and she had really needed to stand her ground and acknowledge her love of God! I asked if she would be prepared to do so if it happened again now? She listened to what I was saying and some of it tied up with her own revelations from Sedona. After much discussion she was able to untangle a lot of her personal issues and free herself up from some of them. I knew there would be more to untangle in the future, but it was certainly a GREAT moment of healing. The following day she went back to look at the picture and was more at ease with it, discovering that most of her fear had gone!

The lesson for me here was that the picture had been the means of helping my friend in a very deep way and it would probably do the same for others, which was why it had come to me. I was beginning to wonder if some of my path in the future would be about reawakening the 'Christ' side of the Trinity in people, for this was certainly what had happened to my friend. Anyway, I decided to put the picture up in the sitting room, not on the main wall, but in a corner where it could be seen if it was needed. I felt this was a good compromise and quite satisfactory!

As the summer continued I became more and more aware that I was being used to remind people of what Jesus had done and why He had done it. In some way I seemed to be bringing Him back into people's consciousness. Many people who came to see me were wonderful spiritual beings but had not seen how they were hanging on to controlling their lives with an iron grip, instead of giving themselves into the hands of the universe/God and 'dying' to themselves. They were lacking a part of the 'peace, which passes all understanding' which comes from being 'born only of God'. I thought back to my hundreds of conversations with my youngest son and how his true turning point had been when he had accepted, with every ounce of his being, that there was a greater power than himself. I recalled the day he had asked to die to his own self and to serve solely as a vessel for God. I remembered my sister's painful but fruitful experience, my many conversations with Roy and several other conversations and I realised that maybe I had been doing this work already for quite some time. I never for one moment, however, considered labelling myself a Christian again. Jesus himself lived unlabelled in the 'pre-Christian' era. He was known purely as 'the son of God'. My own path is truly an unlabelled one and encompasses and embraces ALL.

I had occasion, towards the end of the summer to call on Derek, the interfering acquaintance that I have mentioned several times before. As I approached his house I could feel such blackness around it that I didn't really want to go in. I pulled myself together and made my self overcome my fears and of course everything was fine. He was out at the time but I had a good conversation with his wife and felt quite comfortable. As I left the house, I wondered again about the black energy and the growing strength of it and I prayed earnestly for the highest good to sort it out. I did not know why I was feeling the black and to be honest I felt rather puzzled!

In September 2007 the farmhouse was nearly complete. The plumbing and electrics were finished and there were only about three more areas still to paint. We had one marvellous sunny weekend, when the farmhouse hosted a reunion of all the ladies who had been in Sedona with me. All the rooms were let out for two nights and it was a great test of all the work that had been done. We only had one flood from an old pipe, which wasn't too disastrous! I was looking forward to going shopping in the near future, spending what was left of the donation on all the finishing touches that we needed, such as pictures, bedding, furniture, rugs, carpets, kitchen equipment etc. Everyone who came to visit the house marvelled at its transformation and I was indeed very, very happy.

So life seemed to be unfolding nicely, the project was well underway, relationships between us all were at an all time high and life was rosy! But the universe, as it so often does, had a surprise up its sleeve that I had not seen coming. Thank goodness I didn't, because I only just survived it!

19

Healing a past life

at its very core

THE EVENTS THAT BROUGHT ME to the climax of this story started in mid September 2007, with that unfortunate acquaintance of ours, Derek. I had already been trying to avoid him for some months, partly because of the black energy I felt around him and partly because I did not feel he was a very honest person. I really wanted as little to do with him as possible. However, he suddenly foisted himself upon me in a way that I was unable to ignore because for reasons best known to himself, he tried to interfere, yet again, with matters that did not concern him. My eldest son was with me when the first really serious event took place and after he had heard a little of what Derek had to say, he spoke vociferously on my behalf, realising how unjustly I was being spoken to and Derek walked away. However, Derek unfortunately, could not leave me alone, and came and confronted me for a second time a few hours later, when he knew I was visiting a mutual friend. I was flabbergasted at some of the things he was coming out with and unfortunately, allowed myself to get very angry. My anger came from the fact that he was denying some of the very thoughtful things that I had done for him in the past. We had quite a heated argument as I tried to defend myself and the more I argued the more he towered over me in a real rage. On two occasions I thought he was going to hit me, but he didn't. It was a very frightening experience, not just having a big angry man standing threateningly over me but because I could not comprehend how such an intelligent man should twist everything I said. His unkind accusations, and having my generosity denied in front of a mutual friend was something I could hardly believe was happening. I decided I must get right away from Derek so I backed out of the friend's garden saying as I went that he must leave me alone and that I never wanted anything more to do with him.

The next day Derek's son came to my front door with a fattish brown envelope which obviously contained a lot of paper. I started trembling with fear as I reached out for it, so I decided to leave it on the kitchen table while I went for a walk. During the walk I considered what my best course of action would be regarding the envelope, bearing in mind my immediate adverse reaction on simply receiving it. I eventually decided that it would be wisest to burn it without reading the contents, thereby avoiding any further upset to myself and also confirming my decision to have nothing more to do with Derek. This may sound a bit extreme but I had been so dreadfully upset by him that I didn't want to risk having any further problems until I was feeling more stable. I had turned a blind eye to Derek so many times in the past and had forgiven him for so many other previous hurts, that I really felt that this time we should forgive each other one last time and then go our separate ways in life, wishing each other the best, as we did so. Therefore when I reached home, I burnt the letter, made sure there was only forgiveness in my heart, and tried to think no more about it.

However, unfortunately, the upsetting events had taken a firm grip on my thought processes. This was made worse by the fact that our mutual friend rang me to say she had also received the same letter from Derek. She briefly outlined its contents over the phone and immediately I knew that I had been absolutely right in my decision not to read it. The following morning (which was a Friday) I started to have panic attacks interspersed with sickness and diarrhoea. I kept having dreadful visions of a man towering over me and being powerless to do anything about it. I knew it didn't just relate to my recent experience but that there was also a memory being dragged up from the past life, which was of a man towering over me just before I was put on the bonfire. I was terrified! My elder son tried to calm me down and I tried to calm myself down and I hated myself for being so badly affected. We both knew the problems weren't really mine so why was I not able to let it all wash over me? I had a terrible stomach ache and could hardly eat any lunch but as my aunt was with us I made a brave attempt. I then took the dogs out for a walk and as I appeared to be slightly better my elder son decided to go back to work. But towards the evening the stomach ache started to get worse and worse. My younger son, who was the only person with me at the time, took me to casualty where they diagnosed possible gallstones. I was given some pain killers and told to visit my G.P on Monday. On the way home I was thinking to myself that although the pain may well be caused by gallstones it could also be due to the massive upset from a couple of days ago. By eleven o'clock that evening I was in so much pain that a doctor came out to see me at my home and he gave me a morphine injection. He also decided I might have gallstones but he acknowledged that the pain could also be caused by tension and he too told me to go and see my doctor on Monday.

The pain did not allow me to get much sleep that night, as it had only been dulled by the morphine. I therefore started to work hard on myself to try and find out why this was happening to me. I picked up a book entitled 'Heal Yourself' which was written by Louise Hay, which gives suggestions as to why you might be suffering certain symptoms and can be very accurate. I looked up gallstones but didn't really feel that what she wrote about them made much sense for me. I looked up 'pain', but that didn't really resonate with me either!

The next morning I could do very little except sip water so Edward had to look after the farm. My thoughts were going round and round as I tried to relax my tummy muscles and use visualising techniques to make myself better. Nothing seemed to work and eventually I had the idea of looking inside myself (psychically) to see what was going on. To my horror, when I looked in, I knew that I was looking at the dreaded bonfire from my life as a witch. This was the first time in this life that

I had ever seen it! It wasn't a raging fire as one might have supposed, it was just some dying embers with a few random pieces of smoking stick-ends scattered around. All I wanted to do at that moment was to get it OUT of me! I visualised, I prayed, I could not move until I felt it was moving out of my body. Then, when I thought it was out, I presumed the pain would leave me immediately but to my unbelievable disappointment, it didn't.

I spent the rest of the day asking to know what this was all about and trying to cope with the pain. We rang the doctor for some more advice but they just said that gallstones were very painful, However once they had passed I would feel much better. During the next night, while I was trying to clean myself with white light and love, I was asking God constantly for help. I was delighted that the bonfire was out of me but I couldn't seem to get any further. The following day, which was a Sunday, my husband came over to support my son as it was all getting very distressing. I was keeping the pain at a manageable level by constant white light cleansing and using visualisation of all different types. We almost phoned for an ambulance at one stage but I didn't want to make any unnecessary fuss and decided I could hang on until I saw the doctor the next day.

Well, I did hang on but the doctor who saw me in the local surgery took one look at me and rang the hospital, asking them to admit me straight away as I had been in pain for quite a long time. My sister drove me straight to accident and emergency in a neighbouring town where I underwent a series of tests, after which I was eventually admitted onto a ward in order to have a scan.

Due to pressures on the National Health Service I didn't get booked for the scan until the following morning so I continued to use my practised visualising techniques while I waited, with quite good effect. I managed to get through the night without pain killers but by this time I was on a drip and being given strong anti-biotics as a precaution. By the time the doctor came to see me the following afternoon I was feeling as if I might be getting on top of the pain, so I was very surprised when he said I needed an immediate operation to have my appendix removed. He said there was a terrible mess inside me, showing up on the scan and they felt they should have a look inside me without delay! I was only given a few minutes to take this in (appendix never having been mentioned by anyone until this point) and I was just wondering whether to chance healing myself when the nurses arrived to take me to theatre. I could only think that the universe had arranged this so quickly so I would not have time to do anything other than go along with the doctors plans, so that is what I did!

I won't go into details of the tremendous pain after the operation but it suffices to say that I couldn't get enough pain killers! By the following morning I was feeling a little better and started to eat a tiny bit. The surgeon came to see me and told me I was a very strong woman. He said there had been such a mess inside me, that an operation that normally took one hour had taken four! My appendix, he thought, had been burst for about four to five days and had turned gangrenous inside me. He expected that I would either need a second operation or a drain from my stomach in due course, because he hadn't been able to get all the infection out.

He said would wait and see how I was during the next few days and where the remaining gangrene collected before making a decision. After he left I went into a complete panic. The thought of undergoing another operation after the pain of the last one was unbearable. I didn't like the sound of the drain much either. So I started to ask for God's help almost frantically. I prayed and prayed as I lay in the bed, hardly noticing anyone or anything around me. I hated the thought of gangrene being inside me and I referred to Louise Hay's book again but was really too ill to focus on what it said. When one of the nurses came to change my drip I tried to tell her about the upset a few days before and how I felt my appendix had burst because of it. She didn't have enough time to talk to me and suggested I see a therapist when I was better. None of the nurses had time to talk to anyone; they were all rushed off their feet. I lay there alone with my head spinning, and all the time I could feel my insides starting to swell and burn.

That night the nurses gave me the maximum dose of morphine that I was allowed because the pain was building up so badly. The morphine made me hallucinate so that I hardly knew where I was, but it got me through the night. The whole of the next day I was in so much pain that I can remember wondering if I was going to survive it. My stomach was like an inferno, it was becoming so swollen and the burning sensation was unreal. None of the nurses seemed to realise how awful I was feeling so I requested to see the ward sister. Before she could get to me however, I had a terrible bout of unexpected diarrhoea and the next thing I remember was being rushed into a sideward where the intensive care team gave me a complete overhaul. After many tests and questions they wanted to give me more morphine but I refused because it had made me hallucinate so badly. I don't remember what happened too much after that, other than I sent my sister a text asking her if she could sort out a Will for me. I hadn't made a Will before because of all the uncertainty we had over the farm. My poor sister was beside herself with worry when she got my text, but she managed to get hold of the solicitor and arranged that they would try and make an emergency Will the next day. I somehow felt that the next day would be too late, but I hadn't got the energy to tell her; instead I handed everything over to the universe! As the evening went on I really felt the coming night would be very, very crucial as far as surviving was concerned. I even told the night nurse it was getting to a critical point but I don't think she believed me. My younger son was with me and at the end of visiting hours he said to me,

"Mum, I'm going to set your mobile so you can ring dad by simply pressing this button twice. Then you can phone him during the night if you need to."

He showed me the button and I vaguely took it in. However, his thoughtful action proved to be of enormous value because, if he hadn't done it, it would have changed the course of what happened next!

As the night went from midnight into the early hours of the morning I lay weakly on the bed, feeling the strength leaving me and the infection taking a firm hold. I wondered if I was going to die and if so, why? I was praying all the time, in total communion with God, so much so that I was half out of my body. I felt

His presence everywhere and as we chatted there was calm. I didn't mind if I was dying; I knew it would be a simple transition and I would simply be left looking at my body rather than looking from my body. I was completely reconciled to it, although at the same time very surprised because I hadn't thought it was my time to leave the earth. However by two o'clock in the morning I had given everything up and was left only saying,

"Whatever will be, will be!"

The nurses came in to give me my antibiotic through the drip feed and I hardly felt a thing because I was so at one with the spirit world. The strange thing about being half out of my body was that I knew in advance what was going to happen and what people were going to say! As the nurse spoke to me I felt as if I had already heard her words, it was weird! But that was how I knew I wasn't properly in my body.

I suppose you could call the next hour my 'darkest hour'. It certainly wasn't pleasant and the room I was in seemed pitch black, although my husband assured me afterwards that all the lights were on! The spirits communicated to me that I had a choice ahead of me. They showed me that I had been living in hiding my entire life because I wasn't telling anyone about my real spiritual self. I showed one facet to most of the world and lived another inside. I knew this was true but I hadn't realised that it mattered; in fact I thought I was doing the right thing! I was told that the choice I was being given was to show the world who I really was or to leave my body now, and go back to the spiritual world. I was told they had little use for me as I was at this moment but was being given this opportunity to change. As I lay there, too weak to move or stir much, I tried to take all this in. A vision of my husband came before me and I was made aware that I had never told him about our past life or included him in any of the story, even though he had been so involved in it. I had actually thought my silence was best for him, but anyway, I was now being shown that I had to tell him everything and be honest if I was to continue with this life! I had a vision of the picture of Jesus in my sitting room and I was shown how I had not been brave enough to hang it on the wall it was supposed to go on, I had compromised and put it in the corner. I had known perfectly well where it was supposed to go, I had been told as I bought it! And I knew it was perfectly true that I had not had the courage to follow my instructions. I was shown various other instances where I had blatantly failed to listen to my guiding instinct and I could not deny them.

The minutes ticked by as I allowed these thoughts to go round and round in my head. I remember promising God that I would share the real me with the world in future, that I would stand up and be counted for who I was, and take responsibility for it. I promised I would no longer hide and I would put the picture of Jesus in its rightful place as soon as I could. Then I remembered my mobile phone! I managed to feel for it in the darkness and press the button that my son had shown me, twice. With my heart thumping like mad I spoke to my husband and told him I was fighting for my life. He said sleepily,

"Are you?" and his voice sounded rather surprised.

I don't think anyone in the family had realised just how fast I was deteriorating. However, he said that he would come in to the hospital straight away.

I lay on the bed, knowing I would have to tell my husband everything when he came in. The spirit world was supporting me in every way it could and the burning inferno and the pain inside me was being managed. As I waited, I was shown how I could give my husband a choice. Firstly I would have to tell him the story of the past life and then explain to him that now it was his time to SAVE my life if he wanted to. He would be told that he had taken my life in the past and that it was his chance to put that right, and then his karmic debt would be paid. If I had not been in so much pain and so weak, I would have reasoned that all this was way beyond my husband's current comprehension but as I was pinned with my back against the wall, so to speak, I had to chance it.

I don't know what my husband was thinking as he came to my bedside but he must have been pretty frightened. He came and held my hand and kept saying,

"What can I do?" in an agonised voice, as I lay moaning and groaning.

At this point I felt I had no strength left to fight any more but I could feel the strength in his hand and the love in his voice and it was wonderful. I started to gasp out his part of the story of the past life and how he had put me to death. I made sure he realised that he hadn't known me personally and was just doing his job. I told him that now was his chance to save me and put everything right. I divulged that I had not yet made a Will so if I died the whole farm would go to him and he could live there. Then came the hardest part; I had to tell him that if I lived, he would not be able to live at the farm. We would stay separate, because that was the only way I could do the work that I had to do for the universe. I don't know how much of this he understood and I was far too ill to explain any more than I had. But I knew that he would understand at a deep level and that his soul would benefit from everything that was going on. I held my husband's hand and I said very quietly,

"The choice is yours."

I can't remember if he said anything, I just know he held me so lovingly and gave me his strength throughout the rest of that long night. I knew he was beside himself with worry and that his very presence was keeping me alive. He would have walked away if he hadn't cared.

As we were both coping, in our separate ways, with what was going on, I suddenly blurted out,

"Its time to write the book! I'm being told that I must share this story with the world and it will be used to educate humanity!"

I heard myself promising to God that I would be brave and I would write the book now, as truthfully as I possibly could. This was a terrific surprise to me as I had really thought that writing a book was a bit of a joke before! But the message was very clear and I couldn't deny it.

After an hour or so I felt an excruciating pain building up in my tummy and I wondered what on earth was going to happen. My husband managed to get me up and I perched lob-sidedly on the bed pan in excruciating agony. He held me firmly as I passed an enormous lump of excrement into the bed pan. Slowly the pain started to subside and he managed to get me back on the bed again. I lay there trembling with the effort and enormity of all that was going on but I knew that the passing of the lump was symbolic of the block in my life that had needed to be overcome if I was to carry on living. I also knew the lump symbolized the remains of the BONFIRE and that at last it had gone for ever. A few minutes later, with a certainty that cannot be described, I realised I had just passed the danger point from the infection, and from that moment on, I would start to recover!

The hours and days that followed were physically and spiritually difficult, to say the least. I was indeed on the road to recovery but I had so much to learn that nothing could be hurried. My family were magnificent in their care of me because not only did they man the farm and take care of all my animals, they ensured that someone was with me every minute, day and night, because I was far too weak to look after myself. I was actually frightened of being left on my own because I needed far more assistance than the nurses had time to give me. A commode was put by my bed, for which I was incredibly thankful but I ran the ward out of bed pans at one stage and the nurses had to go round the hospital looking for some more!

It was only two days after my darkest hour that I experienced words and paragraphs flooding out of my brain in the form of a piece of writing. It was as if the book was being put in my head at that moment. I tried to ignore it and it went away but two days later it happened again! I found sentences were forming and ideas for chapters springing up. I knew I was being told that the book had to be written now; not in a few years' time, but definitely now! I was very surprised but I accepted it, so when my sister came to see me and I told her what had occurred, she promised to help me get going with my writing. I was then relieved of the sentence forming, I suppose because I had got the message!

I was kept for quite a while in a state, half out of my body, in which I found I could manage to exist without pain killers. It did get a little confusing at times because I kept thinking that things that were about to happen, had already happened, but it enabled me to stay out of the world of hallucination, and therefore to learn the lessons I had to learn. I knew that when I got a particular awful pain I had a minute or so to get on the commode. Then, once on the commode, I never managed to release the diarrhoea until I stopped fighting, relaxed into the situation, accepting that there was no escape and that it was something I just had to go through. I had no idea that I fought pain so much until this moment, and it was a real struggle to remember that I must simply relax and say,

"Thy will be done!"

But I did learn, I had to, and I think it took three days and countless visits to the commode before it became natural! I was trying to work out why I needed this lesson so badly and thought at the time it may be because I had always shied away from pain (possibly something to do with the bonfire!) instead of accepting that I should experience pain, or not experience pain, at God's discretion, not mine, if I really wanted to work for the highest good. I also had to learn that there is no 'quick fix'. I, selfishly, constantly wanted the whole drama to be over NOW, instead of realising that the highest good is achieved if one lets go and allows the spiritual world to commandeer when it is to be over. Under my control, the highest good would not necessarily be achieved because who am I to know what is needed for the best! These were two big, big lessons for me and I knew that conquering them would really help me cope with my life better and help me in any spiritual work in the future. After this I could look at my life in a more balanced manner and instead of asking for only a rosy outlook, I accepted in advance that - whatever will be will be!

As the days went by and the diarrhoea still did not subside I continued to ask for the reason why, but I stopped panicking over it, accepting I would be told all that I needed to know in due course. Basically, I was accepting, without conditions, that the highest good was prevailing! I became aware of a powerful energy situated in one corner of the ceiling of my room and if I was feeling particularly weak I tapped into it, drawing the strength that I needed. I would visualise breathing it in, allowing it to circulate my body and then breathing out all that I didn't need, until I felt okay. At one stage I remember waking in the night and feeling as if I was receiving a solid downpour of radiation from the corner. I saw it as a strong white light beaming down on my body. I felt hugely encouraged by this and knew I was being looked after and given all the healing and spiritual support that I needed to survive.

I knew my small and large intestine from start to finish by now and all the pains that I had inside were meaningful and taught me more lessons. Unfortunately, I was developing added difficulties because my veins were becoming so traumatised by the constant insertion of needles that they started collapsing, so it was becoming very difficult to keep the drugs and drip working. I desperately wanted to improve enough to start taking the drugs orally. I was also struggling to fight off pneumonia which I felt was imminent because of the phlegm that kept coming up in my throat, making me choke.

One evening, I felt my tummy swelling up again and the burning sensation worsened considerably. I had been waiting all that day for the result of a second scan which would tell the doctors and myself the current state of the infection in my body. As I had to wait for nearly eleven hours for the results, I started to become a bit desperate and I panicked. I just couldn't bare the thought of deteriorating again, which was what I appeared to be doing. The pain got gradually worse and I got into a real state. The nurse came along and gave me a pain killer which made me very sick. My youngest son was becoming very angry with me at this point and said I was being selfish by demanding attention because the doctors had so many other people to attend in the hospital and I should just wait patiently until they could come to me. He said there was something very wrong with the way I was behaving and he had difficulty being in my presence. This shook me to the core because my younger son and I were very close. I struggled into bed and lay uncomfortably on my back, making myself think about what he had said. I gradually managed to take the focus off myself and started to think about other people.

As I did so my tummy started to calm down and within half an hour all my symptoms had subsided. I realised with a shock that I hadn't been getting worse at all, but my state of mind had been so out of control, that I had appeared to be worse.

I then started to realise I had done this same thing to myself when I had allowed Derek to upset me. I had wound myself up into such a bad state that my appendix had burst. It was entirely my own fault for allowing the upset to take such a hold of me. I was totally responsible for everything that had happened to me! This was a revelation indeed.

I looked back over my life and I knew I had always allowed hurt to come right inside me, in this same detrimental way. Sensible people, when they are accused of something they haven't done, simply shrug it off, realising that the problem is not theirs but the other persons. I always allowed the hurt to run riot around my body and cause havoc; on this occasion with disastrous results! I then thought back to my life as a witch and realised why I had this weakness. Of course, I had died in that life, not only resenting the people who had me put to death but also allowing the pain of being accused of things that weren't true to be uppermost in my thoughts. I had obviously been born into this life with the same problem and it had resurfaced in an extreme way now, so that I could see it at root level and resolve it.

After this, I decided I would never again put myself in this position and to build a strong shell that I could put over myself for protection. This shell was shaped like an open mussel and placed over the top of my head.

It would deflect any future attack either side of me and I could choose whether to allow anything in or not, from a safe position. I found myself thinking about my acquaintance and two things struck me. I should really be grateful to him, firstly because his actions were bringing the climax to this story, and secondly, because the lesson I had just learnt was going to be invaluable to me in the future, especially when I started my sanctuary for I would know how to protect myself safely.

I was lying in bed a little later that night, my elder son was with me by this time, when I felt a very bad pain at the beginning of my intestine. My heart sank because I knew that the pain would have to travel round my entire intestine before it all came out as diarrhoea. But, having learnt my lessons well, I didn't fight it at all! I straight away said to myself,

"Thy will be done!"

To my surprise, I felt a little glow in my heart and with the glow came the knowledge that this was the last hurdle. I was about to pass the last problem out of my system.

"Whew!"

My son helped me to the commode and I sat there feeling the pain at the beginning of the intestine. I tried to relax and do all my usual rituals........ Why didn't it shift? I tried everything but nothing seemed to move it. So, I decided to look inside myself (psychically) to see what the problem was. For some reason I felt very nervous and as I looked inside everything was black. I crept down to the bottom of my intestine and there, to my absolute horror, I saw a scaly snake like creature curled up as if asleep but with eyes that were half open. I could hardly bring myself to look at it because I knew it was symbolic of the serpent. However I managed to overcome my fear and glance at it again and I thought,

"What do I do now? How do I get rid of it?"

I became aware that it needed to die but I didn't know how to kill it. I was squirming all over the place; I just wanted it out! In the midst of my discomfort I heard a voice say gently to me,

"Love it. It's the only thing it can't survive."

I shuddered. How could I possibly love it? But I knew I had to try. I thought about loving the acquaintance, Derek, and I found it really hard! I thought about loving all the people who had put me to death in my last life and who had appeared again in this life. Then I thought about loving the serpent that had tempted Eve in the Garden of Eden. I knew that this was an incredibly important moment in my life and felt that if I achieved it I may well be overcoming the root of something big! I looked again at the serpent and eventually found it in myself to love it. And as I sent it love, I saw it dying and I continued to watch it quietly, sending more love, until it was dead. All this time my son had been holding me silently and patiently. I then tried to stand up and as I did so, felt the pain shift a bit. I sat back down again and felt the pain shift slowly right round the many miles of my intestine until it eventually passed right out of me as diarrhoea. It took quite a long time with many stops for rests! Afterwards my whole body felt drained but I knew that was the last of the excrement in my body and it was a terrific relief.

My son managed to half lift me back onto the bed

and I lay there in awe yet again at what had been shown to me. I wondered if it meant that I was now free of original sin or if it was purely symbolic. I really didn't know but I was sure I would find out in due course.

After this, I never had any more diarrhoea. The next day the nurses declared me free of infection. They came and took my isolation signs down and I was allowed out of my room and to shuffle slowly through the ward, getting some exercise. My younger sister came in and helped me to have a wonderful hot bath after which I slept deeply, probably for the first time for two weeks. Later, I decided I could possibly lick a jelly, the first food to even approach my lips for some time, and generally life seemed slightly more tolerable! Even more exciting was the fact that the next day the nurse could not get a new needle in my vein and the old one was desperately infected so they gave up and it was decided I could take my antibiotics orally. Oh joy of joys! I was also told that I HAD TO eat and drink enough by myself because they had taken the drip away too, so I rose to the challenge as best as I could.

In the very weak state I was in, my family still needed to be very attentive during the day time but now left me to cope on my own for a few hours at night. This left much more time for reflection and I'm not quite sure when I became aware of the next thoughts but it was around this time. I was thinking about the acquaintance, Derek, and how he had been so high-handed in my affairs, not just on this last occasion but on many previous occasions. I knew his behaviour was peculiar and I also knew what was going on was his problem and not mine, but I wondered why he had so forced the issue on this last occasion. I thought about the black energy I had felt around his house just before all this had happened and as these thoughts ran through my mind, it dawned on me that he had been brewing up slowly for this incident for some years and that it had been brewing up especially fast during this last summer. My avoidance of him in the last few weeks had obviously been more meaningful than I had realised! Although I had, for some time, suspected that he might be one of the 'gang', I had never been quite sure. Nothing seemed to quite fit into place until it dawned on me that he had been the judge at my trial when I was sentenced to death! Suddenly everything fitted into place like a glove! It explained all his actions towards me and very much how he presented himself to the world in this life. He had sat in judgment over me then and he was doing it again now. Relief flooded through me as I finally understood what had happened. I realised he had behaved the way he had, to bring my last few weeks about, and that now it was done, he would be free to move on and resolve his own issues. I started to thank him at soul level, sincerely and positively. I prayed that he would be able to move on now and I asked for everything possible to contribute towards his highest good. I knew I never wanted anything more to do with him but that was because it was in the best interests of both of us, not because I felt ill will towards him in any way.

A few days after my drips had been removed I was discharged from hospital, and I immediately started to write this book. It feels as if I have been totally guided as to what I should include and only now, as it is drawing to a close, has my phone started ringing again and I find myself coming back into the real world. I believe the purpose of revealing this story to the world right at this moment will show itself in time; I am only concerned that I fulfil my promise to do the Will of God to the best of my ability.

For the last few weeks the universe has been protecting me so kindly and now that people have started phoning me again I realise I am open to being hurt once again. It doesn't matter how or where I put the shell up, someone can get at me around the edge if they want to. I know that if I block myself up totally with a shell it will become impenetrable and I will not be able to receive the guidance for other people that I currently receive. So what to do? I don't want to be a blocked but nor do I want to be hurt and to endanger my life again!

AND GOD THEN GAVE ME
A FULLER UNDERSTANDING!

Because of the way in which I had been unjustly treated and accused in my life as a witch, I had come into this life terrified of people not liking me. Of course I had! It was people (especially the healers who I thought should have known better) not liking me that had sent me to my death! It made such sense to me and now I could see that, I knew why 'HURT' went so deeply within me. I was perfectly balanced over this issue in my last life and the imbalance had only arisen now because of that terrible trial and death! So now, as I realised this, I could WELCOME hurt as part of my growth when it came because I could learn all I needed to learn and

195

afterwards allow any unjustness that was left to go back to its source and resolve itself. Hurrah! I need no longer fear people hurting me! I need no longer fear PEOPLE. I can let go of my imbalance. Now that I know why I wanted everyone to like me, I know why I was so scared to tell anybody who I really was.

And so, the great mystery of life continues.........................

AFTERWORD

Freedom

"A GERMAN WHO LIVED DURING the Second World War has been sent to me. His name is Kohn or Cohen or something. He spent the war helping people of different nationalities get out of Germany. He was a very brave man, a peace-maker who treated everyone as equal. He saved many hundreds of lives. He is an old, old soul. He has been sent to help me out of my difficulties because when he died, he was in similar difficulties. He died before the war ended, before he could be recognised for what he did. He died because he was not brave enough to face what he had to face while he was alive. He died because he was afraid to BE who he really was. He sits near me now, cross legged, arms folded, calmly smoking a pipe, without a care in the world. He's always there. He's helping me release my fears and in doing so, will help release his own………

Feb 2008

Kohn and I, well, we have discovered something. We both always protect our 'core'. We protect it fiercely, thereby not allowing ourselves to love properly or to heal freely. I know WHO I am. But now I want to BE who I am, and to be ABLE to BE who I am, without FEAR. I can't do this myself. I am asking for help – the highest help – Kohn has been sent to me – and the Highest of the High is available to me - I WILL be free!"

March 2008

I feel I have lived this life as a chrysalis. But I can feel the butterfly releasing within me. No-one can hurt me now. Today in meditation I saw many men and women coming at me with knives, spears, muskets etc and they all tried to run me through. But no-one can kill me now. I can only kill myself.

I AM FREE...

Epilogue

"How happy are the single-minded, for the kingdom of heaven is theirs!

How happy are those who know what sorrow means, for they will be given courage and comfort.

Happy are those who claim nothing, for the whole earth will belong to them.

Happy are the merciful, for they will have mercy shown to them.

Happy are the utterly sincere, for they will see God.

Happy are those who make peace, for they will be known as the sons of God.

Happy are those who have suffered persecution for the cause of goodness, for the kingdom of Heaven is theirs."

Matthew, Chapter 5, verse 1...........

About the Author

I LIVE IN A NEWLY converted hayloft on a peaceful one hundred and ten acre farm. The main farmhouse sits across the lawn from my house and has been totally restored to provide extra accommodation. My companions are two dogs, two Dartmoor ponies, three hens, one cat and nineteen sheep. My children pop in and out on a regular basis, and thankfully I have two dear friends who live in my lodge and help me look after it all.

I first started using my healing ability around 1985. Over the years since then I have been privileged to help many people who have found themselves 'stuck' in their lives and through them I have been able to learn and grow as a human being myself. I attribute absolutely everything that happens to a 'higher power' and give thanks on a continual basis for the guidance and support that I receive from this source.

The healing that people (or animals and plants) receive through me is of a very deep nature and always taps into the deepest root of any problem. This can involve unearthing a past life, an experience in this life or simply a chat about 'life' in general. The most important ingredient for success is the total honesty of my clients.

My greatest joy is to bring release to people through healing. Sometimes spirits come to me for help and I find equal joy in helping them to move on. Living life as I do, completely surrounded by nature, I find I am very in touch with 'the other side' and completely at peace.

I currently run a scheme whereby people can come and 'chill out' for a few days on my farm and receive healing if they need to. The property is a naturally healing place and offers restful retreat for those in need. If you would like to know more about me or it, please contact AuthorHouse and they will forward your communication to me.

Milton Keynes UK
Ingram Content Group UK Ltd.
UKHW031029291024
450383UK00001B/14